D0721973

BOOKS BY ANTHONY M. REINACH

The Nature of Puts and Calls
The Fastest Game in Town/Trading Commodity Futures

THE FASTEST GAME IN TOWN / Trading Commodity Futures

Anthony M. Reinach /

THE FASTEST GAME IN TOWN / Trading Commodity Futures

Commodity Research Bureau,Inc.
ONE LIBERTY PLAZA • NEW YORK, N.Y. 10006

Copyright © 1973 by Anthony M. Reinach
Published in the United States by
Commodity Research Bureau, Inc.

Library of Congress Cataloging in Publication Data
Reinach, Anthony M
  The fastest game in town.
1. Commodity exchanges—United States.   I. Title.
HG6046.R43   1975   332.6'328   75-37072
ISBN 0-910418-04-7

Manufactured in the United States of America
First Edition

First Printing Published by Random House, Inc.—1973
Second Printing Published by Commodity Research Bureau, Inc.—1975

To Judy

Contents

THE FASTEST GAME IN TOWN / Trading Commodity Futures

In Wall Street there's a melting pot
Of those who have and who have not
A Rolls Royce or a splendid yacht
Or that well-known proverbial pot.
But each who goes to risk his pay
Looks forward to that golden day
When he may very proudly say:
"I finally made my efforts pay."

1/Where's the Action?

Except during bear market doldrums, the boardrooms of America
bulge with individuals seeking something more than that which can
be gleaned from fixed stares at a busy construction gang. As early as
9:00 A.M. New York Stock Exchange Time, while Californians are
still asleep, men and women from Maine to Miami begin drifting in
to catch early news items or to read current market letters. By 10:00
A.M., the more meticulous "tape watchers" have arrived to view the
"opening." By 11:00 A.M., all the empty seats are occupied and newcomers will already be dotting the outer passageways and wings.
From noon onward, lunch-hour arrivals join the standees. The few
who are customers are easily recognized by their presumptuous shuf-
fling toward the better locations while concomitantly trying to simulate the aura of an institutional account for whom a seat would
surely have been reserved had his arrival but been anticipated.

By 2:00 P.M., which is 11:00 A.M. on the West Coast, the boardrooms in Beverly Hills are more difficult to negotiate than a men's

room at a Green Bay Packer home game during half-time. By 3:00 P.M., some of the New York City traders whose stocks acted nicely that day start to leave, bidding good-byes to their acquaintances with a benevolence that can come only from a self-satisfaction not too consistently enjoyed. At 3:20 P.M., there is a temporary resurgence as anxious executives and uneasy coffee-break employees wander in from the neighborhood to witness the "close" and "run-off." By 4:30 P.M., the customers' galleries have been flushed out except for the debris, but a few stragglers remain in the vicinity of the Dow-Jones and Western Union news tickers hoping for the appearance of an item that will correct the behavior of one of their incorrigible stocks.

Nor are these daily pantomimes acted out solely in the larger urban areas. Each decade, hundreds of new boardrooms are planted in "hinterland" locales where they are expected to soon boast a "productive population pull." By 1980, almost every farm, ranch, and hunting lodge in the USA will be within an hour's automobile ride from the nearest boardroom. Even now at many resorts, widows, dress manufacturers, and financiers alike can be seen forsaking week-day sun rays for the glow of the Trans Lux in boardrooms conveniently installed within walking distance from swimming pools and beaches.

Though some will protest, perhaps even indignantly, that they are but diligent investors, the overwhelming majority of those who cast the boardroom panorama are traders in every connotative sense of the word. Most are "long-side" traders of common stocks. The few who venture onto the unfashionable "short-side" of the market generally do so in consummate silence. There are also those cuff-linked tape watchers who insist they are exclusively interested in shooting for long-term capital gains. But heaven help the brokers who fail to allot them a few shares of the most recent "hot new issue" that quickly spirals to a lusty premium. Naturally, these allotments will be kicked out before the happening of many shirt-to-shirt cuff-link transfers.

Most stock traders borrow money. Some simply trade on "margin," which means borrowing from the brokerage houses that handle or clear their transactions. Some, to increase their "action," borrow from factors or European lending institutions at interest rates considerably

in excess of the genteel 6%. Regrettably, there are also those lar-
cenous few who resort to misrepresentation, and even fraud, in order
that they may achieve or maintain a stock market stake that would
otherwise be out of their reach. Postponing payments and kiting
checks are but part of the game played by these stock market brig-
ands. Some rogues have managed to play the stock market without
any funds whatsoever. But even the fingers of the sanctimonious
have their sticky moments, for how many among them can wholly
resist the temptation to profit just once in a while, and for just a
little bit, from privileged information?

One of the more curious Wall Street phenomena, until the Fed
changed the rules, was the popularity of convertible bonds as trading
vehicles. Had the players gone conservative? Goodness no! Would
you believe? Convertible bonds once enjoyed more leverage and
volatility than their related common stocks. Bankability, you know.

The convertible bond phenomenon dramatized, among other
things, man's speculative hunger and resourcefulness. Shut down his
gambling halls and he will promptly replace them with floating crap
games. I thus never cease to be amazed why so few Wall Street
players have failed to discover the commodity markets. If the name
of the game is "leverage and volatility," Pork Bellies make your
fastest moving stocks resemble, by comparison, prime commercial
paper. And there's always Oats for those who like their action at a
gentler pace. In any event, why pay interest for poor facsimiles of
that which is so abundantly available interest-free?

"I know nothing about commodities," I am told by a trader who
isn't quite sure of the business of the company whose stock he bought
on a tip the day before yesterday.

"Commodities move too fast," I am told by a customers' man
whose financial bible is a service devoted to Wall Street's "fastest
moving" stocks.

"Commodities are too unpredictable," I am told by an elderly
gentleman who has a safe-deposit box stuffed with investments
forced upon him over the years by "unpredictable" lightning-like
price declines that followed in the wakes of their purchases.

"It's more difficult to make long-term capital gains in commodities," I am told by a wealthy lady who just bought a few shares of a "high-flier" for a quick turn.

"You have to be competent to make money in commodities," a ridiculous little fellow once told me. "But the incompetent can make money in the stock market?" I asked in reply.

It is jokingly said that the mistakes of lawyers are incarcerated, the mistakes of doctors are buried, and the mistakes of stock traders are converted into investments. Commodity traders, however, not only have no retreat from reality, they also have but precious little time in which to face and correct their mistakes; for commodity trading metes out justice with impartial speed. In addition, commodity trading metes out justice with a consistency and severity that qualify it as one of the few remaining beacons of integrity in a society taught to regard as dirty words all those antonymous to compassion and mercy, and therein lies the root of most of the objections to trading commodities. A poor commodity-trading performance will not submit to the rationalization: "Under the circumstances, no one else could have done any better." The fact is, many did better *under those very same circumstances.* Nor can a poor commodity-trading performance be buried, nor can it be concealed in a safe-deposit box. A poor commodity-trading performance simply can not be faked out of existence.

Happily, the coin of justice has two sides. In terms of abundance and dispatch, the rewards of a competent trading performance will correspond to the penalties of a poor trading performance. Indeed, by quantitative standards, the potential rewards of competency are virtually unlimited whereas the penalties of incompetency are crucially limited by the trader's bankroll and his psychological capacity to absorb punishment.

Although commodities do not pander to the limitations of traders, they are not without their own limitations. A common stock may often provide the dual function of trading vehicle and investment medium, but a commodity contract would be hard put to qualify as an investment. For one thing, it pays no dividends. More importantly, it can not be long neglected with impunity. The following anecdote partly illustrates the latter limitation:

A lady some years ago, as the story goes, was experiencing considerable emotional strain. When a particular pill provided her with a measure of relief, she gratefully purchased common stock in the pharmaceutical company that manufactured it. But pills, like human beings and commodity contracts, also have their limitations. The stock, alas, was hardly paid for when our prematurely grateful lady suffered a complete nervous collapse. Although expensively institutionalized for over two years, she emerged with a net financial profit. The price appreciation enjoyed by her pharmaceutical stock during that time had more than offset her heavy medical expenses. Such could not have been her fate with a commodity contract.

It is true that a temporarily neglected commodity position has been known to result in a handsome windfall, but a permanently neglected position must result in a delivery, or in a demand for delivery, of the physical commodity subsumed under the positioned contract. Therefore, you would be well advised to execute formal documents instructing the liquidation of all commodity positions upon the advent of institutionalization, kidnapping, perhaps even hijacking, internment in an oxygen tent, death, or any other enforced departure from life's customary streams.

The spectacular profit opportunities available in the commodity market are unique for a combination of three reasons:

1. Price volatility.
2. Leverage.
3. The virtual inevitability that a commodity which goes up comes back down.

1. Commodities generally enjoy a substantially higher degree of price volatility than common stocks. True, there are always some commodities which are temporarily drifting within rather narrow price limits. But there are usually a few commodities on the move—commodities wherein one's stake can be materially altered before the arrival by mail of the initial margin call.

2. Commodities afford unusually high leverage because margin requirements on commodity contracts average but 7½%, and may go as low as 5%. Using a conservative 10% for illustrative purposes, this would mean that a mere 10% price move in a commodity will double the money of those on the right side of that entire move.

Imagine doubling your money in IBM while its shares were merely roaming from $400 to $440, or from $400 to $360. A trader on the right side for the entire move of a commodity that doubled or halved in price would actually enjoy a whopping 1000% profit. Eleven commodities with a speculative following experienced at least one price-doubling move in the 1960's: Cocoa, Copper, Eggs, Orange Juice, Platinum, Potatoes, Pork Bellies, Silver, Soybean Meal, Soybean Oil, and Sugar. Notwithstanding, such moves ought to be regarded as exceptional events—especially those occurring within the life of a single contract. On the other hand, advances or declines of from 15% to 30% are quite common and should offer enough excitement to satisfy even the most action-hungry player.

3. A good common stock that rises to a new price plateau rarely suffers a full retreat to the one from which it was launched, but a commodity that enjoys such a rise will usually retrace its entire advance. For instance, should IBM go from $400 to $800, I would not expect to see it back again at $400—or even $500. But were Cocoa to advance from 25¢ to 50¢, I would very much expect its eventual return to 25¢. In the 1950's, every commodity that doubled in price ultimately retraced its entire advance. In the 1960's, the metals were the only exceptions. Yet, by November 1971, even Silver had splashed down to a level with its 1967 launching pad. A commodity short-seller can thus anticipate a fuller play than a stock short-seller. Rampant inflation would materially alter the ball game.

A 54-month round trip:

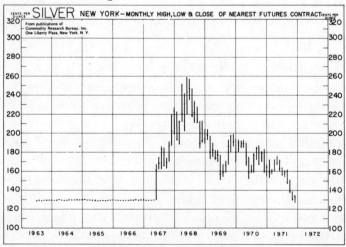

Within four years, twice up and twice almost all the way back down:

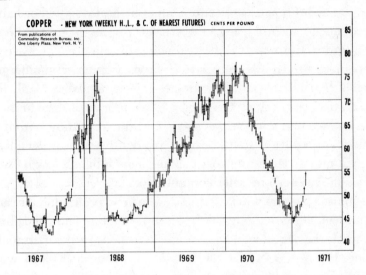

Sometimes what goes up goes all the way back down and then some:

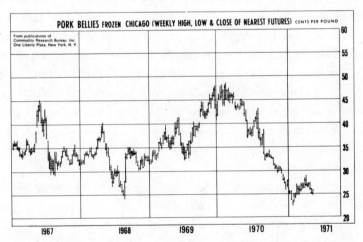

If the unique combination of price volatility, leverage, and "two-way" moves still leaves an unwhetted appetite, pyramiding can be added to the speculative mix. Here's how it might work on the long side:

Suppose you buy 10 commodity contracts and add 1 contract to your position upon each 10% rise in that commodity's price. Should the commodity ultimately double in price, you will enjoy a 1450% profit. If you add 1 contract upon each 5% rise, you will enjoy a 1950% profit. If you add 5 contracts upon the first 5% rise, 4 contracts upon the second 5% rise, 3 contracts upon the next such rise, then 2 and 1 and none thereafter, you will enjoy a 2325% profit. Believe it or not, these are relatively conservative pyramiding approaches. At the aggressive extreme, which is realistic only as a mathematical possibility, the doubling of your position upon each 10% rise will see your initial stake, by the time the price of the commodity doubles, sprout to over 100,000% of its original size.

A pyramid is structured to preclude, hopefully, the necessity to increase its builder's initially committed stake. Consequently, additional margin money was not required for the positional extensions in the foregoing hypothetical illustrations. In fact, money could have been withdrawn in each case except in the one at the aggressive extreme.

What I have written about pyramiding is by no means original. This is what Morton Shulman wrote in his book, *Anyone Can Make a Million*:[1] "As an example of how this low margin requirement can produce spectacular profits, examine the situation if one had bought sugar futures just before the Cuban crop failure a few years ago. At that time sugar prices jumped all the way from 2¢ a pound up to 12¢. Each contract which had been worth $2,200 zoomed all the way up to $13,200. If $200 had been deposited as initial margin, it would have grown to be worth $11,200—an increase of over 5,000%. Furthermore, if pyramiding of the original $200 investment had been fully followed, the $200 would have grown within six months to $5,000,000!"

Pyramiding approaches, other than judicious ones, are intended as just hypothetical illustrations. Among other things, margin requirements are invariably increased at an accelerated rate in the wake of rising prices attended by broadening speculative activity. More importantly, an over-extended pyramid will collapse under the stress of the first market recalcitrance, and even an apparently sturdy pyramid can suddenly crumble into a ruinous heap unless its maintenance has embraced those two crucial concomitants of

[1] Morton Shulman, *Anyone Can Make a Million*, McGraw-Hill, 1966, page 189.

sound judgment—vigilance and caution. Richard D. Donchian, whose "trend timing" studies are widely followed, tells this hair-raiser:[2]

"A member of the Board of Trade, who is allowed to carry positions on lower margin than non-members, decided correctly in December 1960 that Soybeans were ready to move up. Starting with $1500, he increased his position as fast as his equity would allow. By late February, his position had increased to 2 million bushels and his equity to over $190,000. His pyramid was so extended, however, that a 10¢ dip would wipe him out. Perhaps you can guess what happened. From February 28 to March 13, Soybeans, which had risen nearly a $1.00, settled back about 30¢. The Board of Trade member did not run for cover quickly enough and wound up owing his broker around $10,000. Since then, he has been selling mutual funds."

As much leverage as the long-side pyramider enjoys, the short-side pyramider enjoys even more; for *margin requirement reductions escort a declining commodity* at roughly the pace margin requirement increases escort an advancing commodity. Also, market recalcitrance is empirically less apt to threaten a pyramid erected on a declining commodity than one erected on an advancing commodity. Therefore, a short-side pyramid builder enjoys the additional advantage over his long-side colleague of either being able to fashion his structures with greater aggressiveness, or of being able to maintain a correspondingly extended structure with greater peace of mind.

By reason of the exciting moves that are such a unique hallmark of CMA,[3] it's indeed difficult to find a year, a month, or even a week which is totally devoid of stranger-than-fiction dramatics in at least some commodity.

Take 1963: Cocoa was just a trading affair, Copper was dormant, and Pork Bellies were still a bore. Lead, however, was enjoying its first 6 months of an 18-month bull market; Hides were in a clear-cut

---

[2] Richard D. Donchian, Vice President, *Commodity Commentary*, Hayden, Stone Inc., July 23, 1968.
[3] Commodity Market Action.

downtrend; and (World) Sugar almost tripled in price, suffered a severe collapse, and then recovered—all within 10 months.

Take 1964: This was Copper's year—from 30¢ to over 60¢, and then back to under 40¢. There was also plenty of action in Cottonseed Oil, Potatoes, Rye, and even in the habitually tranquil Oat market. Bears had their best play in May Wheat.

Take 1965: This was the year Cocoa plunged to 10¢ and then doubled back up to 20¢; but most of the longs who rode the advance seemed to be those who had stubbornly stayed on the hook during that "impossible" final plunge. Hides were in an extended bull market and Copper fluctuated widely and wildly. May Potatoes provided plenty of excitement by soaring beyond $6.00. The real excitement, though, was the debut of Pork Bellies as a speculative favorite —thanks to their smart advance from 30¢ to 55¢. Rabbis couldn't eat them, but more than a few were known to be trading them.

Take 1966: May Pots[4] were back in the limelight by rising to over $5.00. Copper, Cottonseed Oil, and Eggs also enjoyed fine moves; but the Soybean outperformed them all, experiencing its most exciting bull market in a dozen years. Its sudden price collapse, sadly, sent many budding geniuses back to common stocks.

Take 1967: Although Sugar opened the year by plummeting to a 25-year low, Silver was soon to monopolize the headlines. From a mundane government-controlled item, this traditionally popular coinage metal abandoned its price captivity to blossom into a trader's delight. With Silver leading the way, even Cotton summoned the courage to thumb its nose at price-shackling influences. Wheat was again a joy to the bears.

Take 1968: Led by Wheat, which retreated to pre-World War II price levels, grains sunk as if determined to wrap up the farm states for the Republican Party. This election year was also featured by some dynamic two-way action in Cocoa, Orange Juice, and Silver. Pork Bellies finally retraced the full extent of their exciting 1965 price advance.

Take 1969: A bull market year for Copper, Eggs, Pork Bellies, and Rapeseed. A bear market year for Oats, Orange Juice, Platinum, and Sugar. A two-way year for Beef Cattle, Broilers, Silver, and Soybean Oil.

---

[4] Potatoes.

Take 1970: This was the year the Corn blight generated excitement not only in Corn, but also in most of the other grains. Some of the excitement even rubbed off on Eggs and the meat products. Soybean Oil reached a 14-year high and Sugar a 7-year high. But it was an unhappy year for bulls in Cocoa, Copper, and Wool. There was no blight in Ghana—just a few Swiss financial playboys who hoped there'd be one; the only blight on the Copper picture was a Marxist incursion in Chile that barely tweaked this metal's downside price behavior; and Australian sheep, being never healthier, saw prices for their coats recede to pre-New Deal levels.

Take 1971: Sugar faded after scaling $5.00 early in the year, but suddenly regained its color around Thanksgiving and was roaring beyond $8.00 by New Year's Eve. Cocoa remained a timid bear, but Cotton and Orange Juice became rampant bulls. Lumber and Plywood dramatically qualified as hot trading items. And, interestingly, Futures Trading had not only surpassed New York Stock Exchange trading, it was surpassing it by almost 50%.

Take 1972: After dismal prices for the 1971-1972 Potato crop, tropical storm Agnes sent prices for the 1972-1973 Potato crop soaring. Platinum (thanks to the anti-pollution craze) and Wool made spectacular comebacks. Sugar climbed over $10.00 and Cotton nudged 44¢, but they had been there before. The Russians sent Wheat over $2.00 for the first time in almost a decade, Soybeans rose above the magic $4.00 figure, and inflation wreaked havoc with meat and wood product prices. Even Soybean Meal scored new all-time high prices. For overall volatility performance, the Pork Belly again walked off with the Oscar.

Take January to May 1973: As with June in Rodgers & Hammerstein's Carousel, commodity prices busted out all over. New plateaus were reached in Cattle, Cotton, Hogs, Lumber, Plywood, Pork Bellies, Potatoes, Rapeseed, Silver, Soybeans, and Soybean Meal. The forecasts in Chapter 12 were materializing while this book was being set in type. But New York and American Stock Exchange seat prices were impervious to inflation. By late March, a New York Stock Exchange seat was selling for less than a Chicago Mercantile Exchange seat and an American Stock Exchange seat was selling for less than a Chicago Board of Trade seat.

Take the future: No one knows for certain which commodities will be providing the most action at any particular time, but it is easy to predict that there will at most times be enough CMA to keep the more serious players occupied.

Before examining specific action characteristics, let's look in on a typical week in the life of a commodity trader—to absorb the mood of commodity trading and to grasp some of its jargon.

Meet "Shorty" Long who trades in Wheat,
 And Soybean Oil and Meal;
In others, too, where he believes
 He has a market feel.
But at those times when Shorty's faced
 With a distressing loss,
It's heart that keeps him in the role
 Of his own lonely boss.

2/Action of a Commodity Trader

Our hero is "long"[1] 12 May[2] Pork Bellies at an average cost of 43¢.[3]
His position amounts to $185,760[4] of the product from which bacon
is made, which is a lot of bacon. Shorty's cash outlay, however, is
only $9000,[5] or about 4.9% of his total contractual commitment.
Happily, May Bellies are up over 3¢ from Shorty's average purchase
price. In fact, they closed the previous Friday at 46.12.[6] Before
deducting commissions,[7] his paper profit exceeds $13,000.[8] Then
why, at 5:50 A.M. on a cold wintery Monday morning in a New York
City suburb, is Shorty wide awake? Let's listen in as his mind begins
to function:

---

[1] The terms *long* and *short* do not denote the same proprietary relationship in commodity futures trading as they do in securities trading. For instance, being long 5M
(five thousand) bushels of May Wheat constitutes the ownership of one contract that
requires its owner to *take* delivery of 5M bushels of Wheat (of a specified grade) sometime in May, unless the contract is priorly sold. Being short 5M bushels of May Wheat

Monday—5:55 A.M. "Four hours and thirty-five minutes before the opening in Chicago.[9] Why in heaven's name can't I sleep? Perhaps it was that nervous close Friday. Or was it a nervous close? Is it just I who's nervous? Low volume all day with the Mays trading up a quarter to 46.37. Slightly over 5000 contracts until 1:30 P.M. Certainly not very many. And then bang—2000 contracts in the last half hour with the Mays selling back to Thursday's close. Traders evening up before the weekend? Nonsense! Why weren't the shorts as anxious to even up?"

Monday—7:30 A.M., on a parkway headed toward Manhattan's financial district. "One does miss the traffic at this hour. Bellies are not only ruining my sleep, they're also hurting my marriage. My wife's right. I didn't hear a thing she said all weekend. Maybe I should trade Oats instead. Those market letters[10] are hollering 50¢ for Bellies. How stupid can I get? I should know better than to listen to those letters. At least listening to my wife doesn't fog my market judgment. But not just the brokerage house touts, the entire trade[11] is bullish. Then who did the selling at Friday's close?"

Monday—9:30 A.M., while standing at a commodity news ticker machine. "Another bullish blurb by that hot[12] Western outfit: ('A close over 46.70 for May Bellies will herald the next important upthrust. If that eventuality materializes, and we think it will,

---

also constitutes the ownership of one contract, but a contract that requires its owner to *make* delivery etcetera.

[2] In commodity futures trading, each commodity has certain designated delivery months for which contracts may be purchased. In Pork Bellies, those months are February, March, May, July, and August.

[3] Pork Belly prices are quoted in cents per pound. Each contract prior to the February 1971 contract called for the delivery of 30,000 pounds. Beginning with the February 1971 contract, the quantity was increased to 36,000 pounds.

[4] The figure $185,760 is arrived at by the following computation: 12 (contracts) $\times$ 43 (cents) $\times$ 36,000 (pounds).

[5] The purchase of a commodity futures contract requires a down payment. The term *margin*, borrowed from the vernacular of securities trading, is used to identify this down payment. Margin requirements vary from commodity to commodity and may even vary for some of the delivery months of the same commodity. Margin requirements also change as market conditions dictate, the principal considerations being price level and price volatility. The margin used in this Pork Belly example is $750 per contract.

[6] The minimum fluctuation for Pork Bellies is .025 (1/40) cents per pound or 2½ points. In the vernacular of commodity futures trading, the "½ point" is understood but not spoken. 46.12, therefore, is in reality 46.12½ or 46.125.

look for the 50¢ rampart to be easily scaled.') Here comes the Hog[13] run.[14] It's light. 10% less than last Monday and 5% less than a year ago. Anyway, this should make for a firm Belly opening."

Monday—10:10 A.M., on a telephone to a floor-trading member of the Chicago Mercantile Exchange: ('Yes, cash market steady. Not too many Bellies went into storage over the weekend. Weren't the latest slicing figures[15] impressive?') "I wonder when those early spring holidays[16] are going to start putting a crimp in the slicing figures."

Monday—10:20 A.M. "That cash market's a phoney. Those boys[17] might be making private deals 2¢ under the market for all I know. What am I doing trying to sort fact from fiction? I'm only supposed to be a market reader. The devil with the market! It's platitude time:

'Markets aren't one-way streets.'
'You can't go broke taking a profit.'
'Sell down to the sleeping point.'

(To his broker): Sell 3 May Bellies at 46.22 or better, good till canceled."

Monday—10:40 A.M. "Bellies look strong as hell. Maybe I should have bought more instead of selling."

---

7 Commission rates are, of course, subject to change. In this illustration, round-trip commissions are $45 per contract.

8 Assuming Shorty Long's paper profit to be 3.125¢ per contract (46.125 minus 43), his total paper profit before deducting commissions amounts to $13,500. This is arrived at by the following computation: 12 × 3.125 × 36,000.

9 Pork Bellies trade on the Chicago Mercantile Exchange from 10:30 A.M. to 2:00 P.M., Eastern Time.

10 The clarions of brokerage house wisdom.

11 Those in the *alleged* "real know."

12 The term *hot*, in this and similar contexts, generally connotes: "On the record as being unequivocally right approximately once in a row." Whether or not the subject judgment was backed with money is totally immaterial.

13 A Pork Belly comes from the underside of a Hog.

14 Number of Hog arrivals at designated market places.

15 A reasonable reflection of the demand for bacon may be ascertained from the bacon slice in conjunction with storage figures (see footnote 20).

16 Bacon has gallantly borne the stigma of being religion's all-time number one dietary no-no.

17 Those *in* the "real know."

Monday—10:45 A.M. "All three off at 46.27. A good execution for a change. There they go. 46.45 for the Mays. I always seem to get good executions on orders I shouldn't have entered in the first place."

Monday—1:58 P.M. "Bellies again selling off at the close with the volume picking up. Something's fishy in this market. Wish I had sold more. Too late now."

Monday—2:30 P.M., back at Shorty's office. "With May closing down on the day (45.95), my sale looks good. Then why am I uptight? I was more relaxed two months ago when I had 15 Febs[18] at a half-cent loss. I guess I dug that market, but don't dig this one. Another evening of deaf ears for my wife. Better bring her some flowers, and don't forget to ask for one of her sleeping pills."

Tuesday—9:45 A.M. "Damn! A large Hog run. Maybe that's why the market was so weak at yesterday's close. Well, a quarter lower at the opening isn't too serious. Let's hope it's no more than that. It should soon rally back and give me a chance to unload 3 more. (To his broker): Sell 3 May Bellies at 45.97 or better, good for the day only."[19]

Tuesday—10:45 A.M. "Not as bad an opening as I had feared, and look at them rally back: 45.80. 45.90. 45.95. 45.92. 45.97. 46.02. 46.00. 46.05. 46.10. Those Hog run openings are getting to be sucker traps. There's still plenty of life in Bellies, and I've only got 6 left. Am I selling too soon?"

Tuesday—2:05 P.M. "Boy, what a close! 46.45 on May. Could I be wrong? Is it possible they're going to 50¢? That Soybean Oil is getting to look interesting. Should I buy a couple to get the feel?"

Wednesday—6:30 A.M. "The world still sleeps and I'm wide awake. Serves me right for not taking a sleeping pill last night. Oh my Lord, I forgot! The monthly storage figures[20] are due out after today's close. They were bullish last month, which makes them

[18] February Pork Bellies.

[19] There is a wide variety of ways in which commodity orders can be entered. This subject will be examined in Chapter 6.

[20] Storage figures are reported daily, weekly, and monthly for both Chicago and non-Chicago warehouses. The monthly figures have great potential market impact. Storage figures, in conjunction with the bacon slice (see footnote 15), provide a reasonable reflection of bacon demand. Storage figures, in conjunction with the Hog population, provide a reasonable reflection of future bacon supply.

a favorite to be bearish this month. Either way, I think the market's reaction will be short-lived. It's how full the pipe lines[21] are that counts. But at this level of the market, a bearish report could have more immediate impact than a bullish one. There I go, thinking like an analyst again. The market itself tells all the story I need to know. Repeat three times you dumdum: The market itself tells all the story I need to know. The market itself tells all the story I need to know. The market itself tells all the story I need to know. Will today be the day the market tells me to run for cover? To hell with Soybean Oil until Bellies are off my mind."

Wednesday—10:15 A.M. "Early morning figures seem pretty neutral. Why phone that guy in Chicago? All he knows is what others feed him. I think I'll just sit tight for a while and let the market do the talking."

Wednesday—12:30 P.M. "Some firm market! There go the Mays to 46.75. A close here or higher will have every chart boy on the bandwagon. Could this market be discounting a bullish storage report? Two months in a row? I don't believe it. Is it a crime not to have a position? Okay, let's see whether they'll take me out at 46.77. (To his broker): Sell 6 May Bellies at 46.77 or better, good today only."

Wednesday—12:40 P.M. "46.72. 46.75. 46.70. 46.67. 46.65. Maybe I was too piggish. Should I lower my price, or just put the damn things in at the market? No, I think I'll wait a bit longer."

Wednesday—12:50 P.M. "46.70. 46.67. 46.75. 46.77. 46.80. 46.77. 46.80. 46.77. 46.85. 46.92. There they go, and I was worried about my price. Could have put them in higher. Anyway, now I'll be able to get some sleep. Can also be an attentive family man for a change. Holy Mackerel! It's Billy's birthday tomorrow. What kind of a baseball glove was it he said he wanted?"

Wednesday—1:35 P.M. "Watch that market churn. It's been getting

---

[21] From Hog to consumer's plate is a long route with quite a few stopovers. The Hog population and warehouse storage figures can be reasonably ascertained. How much bacon resides with wholesalers, retailers, and in the refrigerators of restaurants and housewives cannot. For this and other reasons the Pork Belly market often acts in contradiction to apparent, visible, or evident fundamental factors. Needless to say, such recalcitrance crops up in all markets with unpredictable frequency, to varying degrees, and for a wide diversity of reasons.

nowheres for over half an hour. And that volume; already 11,800 contracts. With the closing activity to come, there'll be 15,000 contracts traded today. This has to be the turn."

Wednesday—1:40 P.M. "Market still getting nowheres. If the storage report is bullish, tomorrow's opening will be the time to sell. If bearish, now's the time. How big a short position should I consider? 10? Certainly no more than that. All 10 now, or 5 now and 5 at tomorrow's opening if the report is bullish, or 5 now and 5 on the first rally if the report is bearish? Best be cautious. (To his broker): Sell 5 May Bellies at the market."

Wednesday—1:55 P.M. "46.82 on all 5. Ticked down there once and bounced right back to 46.90. It's tough to get a good execution on market orders during hectic trading, but why am I always the one to end up with the low eighth?"[22]

Wednesday—2:03 P.M. "That execution is getting to look better all the time. Watch those Bellies fade. The Mays are down to 46.67. Someone sure dumped in a hurry."

Wednesday—2:30 P.M., while alternating between his seat, the water cooler, and the commodity news ticker—waiting for the storage report. "This is more nerve-racking than when the kids were born. Lord, don't let me forget Billy's baseball glove."

Wednesday—2:45 P.M. "Maybe I'm rooting the wrong way. Perhaps I should be rooting for a bullish report so I can sell more at tomorrow's opening. But what if they go through the roof?"

Wednesday—2:50 P.M. "Who am I to be bearish when the rest of the world is bullish? Except, of course, that guy who dumped at the close today. Or was it more than one guy?"

Wednesday—2:55 P.M. "I couldn't leave well enough alone. I just had to have a position. It will serve me right when they're up the limit[23] tomorrow."

Wednesday—3:05 P.M. "Here it comes. It's bearish, real bearish. I knew it all along. Damn! I should have shorted all 10 this afternoon. Platitude time:

[22] The terms *low eighth* and *top eighth* are borrowed from the securities' vernacular, stocks customarily being traded in eighths.

[23] Commodity futures have limits beyond which they cannot trade during any one daily session. The limit on Pork Bellies is 3¢ or 300 points, 150 points up and 150 points down.

'Half a loaf is better than none.'

'Bulls and bears make money, but pigs never do.' "

Thursday—10:35 A.M. "Would you believe? They're opening down the limit. And here I sit like a dummy, short only 5 contracts. Perhaps they'll rally later."

Thursday—11:05 A.M. "No way. 7000 contracts offered down the limit. Guess that's it for today. Might as well go back to the office and catch up on some desk work. Why can't my brilliant wife balance her own checkbook?"

Friday—10:45 A.M. "Another 75 points down. No sense shorting any more even if they do rally. Better start thinking about where to cover. What's the next support level? Who's got the chart book?"

Friday—11:15 A.M. "That Soybean Oil is so quiet—like those calms in the South Pacific before a tropical storm. Oil must be getting ready to go. (To his broker): Buy 3 July Oils at 8.32 or better, good till canceled."

Friday—11:35 A.M. "Didn't take me long to pick up that Oil; and at 8.31, a point below my bid. Beware of gifts from Greeks and floor brokers. Am I being fooled by this market?"

Friday—5:00 P.M., in a traffic jam headed for the suburbs. "That Oil looked sick. What a miserable close (8.27)! Bellies don't give me enough of a headache. I need a bigger one. Think I'll kick that Oil out Monday, first thing. I hope Billy liked his glove, but what does he need with a baseball glove in mid-winter anyway? Which reminds me: I wonder how that blizzard in Iowa is going to affect the Hog run Monday?"

Shorty Long is an inquisitive, enterprising, and adventurous individual. Most commodity traders are. Beyond this, the similarities begin to diminish. The combination of risk capital available, psychology, temperament, and other attributes varies from trader to trader. As a consequence, some prefer the fast movers like Pork Bellies. Others prefer the quiet Oats. Some prefer the short side of the market. Others wouldn't be short with Chinese money. Some go after quick profits. Others seek bigger plays. Still others confine themselves to the search for long-term capital gains. Thus, even if our fictitious hero were real and eager to teach the art of trading commodities profitably, he would still be powerless to transform any one particular person into a successful trader—no matter how hard he tried. However, the knowledge and experience of the world's Shorty Longs should serve as invaluable short-cuts to success.

Another important dissimilarity of commodity traders is the time they are able and willing to devote to this pursuit. Quite a few devote their entire vocational lives to commodity trading—making hundreds of trades every year. Many more devote but portions of their lives to commodity trading. Some may make but one or two trades a year, or even go a few years without making a single trade. Therefore, a professional operating on the floor of the Chicago Mercantile Exchange must necessarily approach commodity trading differently from the busy lawyer or executive. Notwithstanding, the principles applicable to profitable commodity trading are just as valid for the occasional trader as they are for the active one. The variable is simply the number of profit opportunities encountered.

Legendary speculator Jesse Livermore once said that he would have been consistently wealthy throughout his life had he but limited his market plays to no more than four a year. Obviously, such market discipline would have enabled Livermore to avoid many of the pitfalls into which over-active traders often plunge. Accordingly, if you can afford to invest the time for even one market play a year, why not try commodities?

It's strange, indeed, with eyes in place
Where onward they must always face
That man's hindsight is far more right
Than ever was his best foresight.

3/What's the Action?

Trading commodity contracts is a productive pursuit; productive,
that is, to the extent you profit from it. Betting on the ponies is not.
Nevertheless, a type of race-track betting action that is not at all
uncommon illustrates the essence of market action—be it commodity, common stock, used car, or some other.

Many who frequent horse races know not an owner, trainer, or
jockey, have no friends who can boast such relationships, never bet
on tips, and can glean but superficial knowledge from form sheets.
Yet, some of these people are able to wager with a fair degree of
success. How do they do it? There are probably several ways. Here
is one of them:

Your attention, we shall suppose, is one day captured by a sleek-looking filly named Fleetfoot. She goes off at 20 to 1 and breezes
along to come in fifth, six lengths behind the winner. You wonder
how she would have done had she been really trying. You figure
her 20 to 1 price was occasioned by the fact that she was just out

for the exercise and, accordingly, you make a mental note to follow Fleetfoot's future performances—with emphasis on *the betting action that precedes those performances.*

On her next outing, Fleetfoot goes off at 15 to 1, seems to try a little harder, and comes in fourth. Although you figure she was not this time entirely out for the exercise, you also judge that her owner or trainer had considered her as having been "not quite yet ready." But, for the first time, a queer nervous excitement, triggered by some unidentifiable knowledge, has you eagerly awaiting Fleetfoot's next appearance.

On this anxiously anticipated occasion, against the same class of competition, the morning line on Fleetfoot is 15 to 1. At the track, however, the odds open at 8 to 1 and gradually work down to 5 to 1. The betting action seems to scream that Fleetfoot is "ready." "This must be it!" you say to yourself. You go to the window that probably corresponds more to your financial aspirations than to your financial affluence and back your convictions in the belief that, win or lose, you will be getting a good run for your money.

Because CMA is far more complex than race-track action, the clues generated by CMA are many times more numerous. The constant availability of abundant clues requires of the commodity trader much greater mental effort than that which is required of the horse player, but such a generosity of clues correspondingly enables him to be profitably employed on a much more continuing basis. Indeed, a student of CMA can always find additional work to do—search for new clues, re-evaluate old clues, follow new markets, assess the validity of already known clues in respect to these new markets, and so forth. The real test of a trader's ability is, of course, ultimately determined by the results he achieves, but between his preparatory work and the achievement of those results lay countless moments of decision. To try to visualize the scope of one of these moments, let's start with Illustration I, which is generically typical of certain CMA.

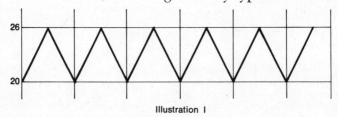

Illustration I

Let us say that Illustration I portrays the fluctuations of imaginary commodity X over a period of a year, and that an imaginary trader has been on the side lines trying to figure out which way X was going to emancipate itself from the well-defined price area to which it had been so long confined. Then one day, he decided that the likely direction of X's forthcoming breakout would be up. What, perhaps, were some of the considerations that influenced him? Maybe, so he gauged, X's action had become increasingly buoyant; or maybe X's action, though not particularly buoyant, had finally halted a long-term downtrend; or maybe his judgment was principally dictated by the fact that recent volume and open interest figures of commodity X had bullish overtones; or maybe his assessment was prompted by one of the many considerations not covered here, or by a combination of two or more considerations. Was this, then, our trader's moment of decision? It would have been for some traders, but for ours it was merely an occasion to intensify his preparation for the arrival of that moment.

The reason our trader's moment of decision has not yet arrived is that most seasoned traders avoid positioning markets in anticipation of breakouts. They claim traders are better off waiting for markets to tell them what to do. This usually means following market moves which are already under way. In so doing, they forgo some profits but reduce the risk of having their trading funds tied up as a result of inaccurate timing. Although the analogy leaves something to be desired, a trader of this persuasion might point out that it certainly would have been wiser to back Fleetfoot on her third outing at 5 to 1 than on her first outing at 20 to 1.

Nevertheless, there are seasoned traders who do position markets in anticipation of breakouts. Because profits bestowed by the initial phases of moves are usually purchased at the cost of timing, such profits are only a minor attraction to these traders. What they consider important is the added confidence enjoyed in markets they have operationally anticipated. As a result, in theory, they will possess the courage to pyramid their initial positions more aggressively and be thereby rewarded for the patience they invested at the outset.

Both market approaches are pregnable to market recalcitrance. If a market move fails to get under way, or gets under way in the wrong direction, only the anticipators are damaged—the followers not yet being in the market. If a market move fails shortly after its inception, mostly the followers are damaged—the anticipators already having a profit cushion. If a market reversal at some later stage of its progress catches a whole host of traders by surprise, the extent of the damage inflicted upon each will depend upon a wide variety of factors. The most crucial of these will be, in each case, the alacrity with which the changed situation can be grasped and, subsequently, upon which it can be acted. Therefore, the fact that both market approaches have been traditionally pursued with fine results testifies not only to the merit of the two approaches, but also to the legendary alertness of seasoned commodity traders.

Our trader, being a follower, waits "positionless" for the breakout. Then, one Friday morning at 11:17 A.M., the breakout (Illustration II) occurs.

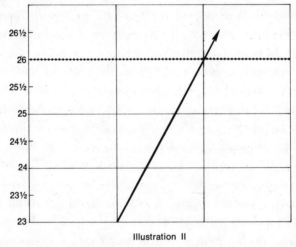

Illustration II

What should our trader be thinking about? Then what should he do? Does the volume confirm or deny the validity of X's breakout, or is it neutral? If X has a history of false breakouts, how likely is this to be just one more of them? If X does not have a history of false breakouts, what are the chances of this being one of the exceptions? At any rate, how seriously should he view a mere ½-point breakout? Should he wait until it becomes a 1-point, 2-point, or 3-point breakout? Or should he position at least a few contracts immediately? Assuming our trader judges the ½-point breakout as "probably" valid, should he jump in now and buy as many contracts as his free trading funds will allow? Or should he buy half now and the other half when the "probability" of the breakout's validity has been translated into a "virtual certainty"? In the latter event, should he buy the second half on the way up or await a "material price reaction"? Also, what constitutes a "virtual certainty" and what constitutes a "material price reaction"? One thing is a certainty: If our trader, upon the arrival of this (or any other) moment of decision, has not preparatorily considered these and other issues, he will either take no action at all or be compelled to act partly on whim.

Our trader, let us say, purchases 5 contracts on Friday morning shortly after 11:17 A.M. Immediately thereafter, he will start being confronted with a series of less critical decisions—but critical ones nonetheless. For instance, how about pyramiding? Should he pyramid haphazardly by adding to his position when the market seems to be at favorable buying junctures, and to extents in correspondence with his "certainty"? Or should he program his pyramiding? Should he buy an additional contract every point up; every 2 points up; or should he buy 2 contracts every 3 points up—until X hits 35; 40; 45; or higher? Or should he add 4 contracts 2 points up, 3 contracts 4 points up, 2 contracts 6 points up, 1 contract 8 points up, and then make no more positional additions? Further, to protect equity, should he issue stop-loss orders simultaneously with the purchase of all contracts, or sometime later on? And how far under the market? To protect growing "paper" profits, should he keep raising extant stop-loss orders? How much and how frequently? Or should he merely rely on mental "stops"?

One of our trader's most critical moments of decision will arrive when he perceives that market clues have begun to shift their weight in favor of X's sale. In preparation for this moment, our trader should have asked himself such questions as: How large a rise is X likely to experience? Which clues will be the probable candidates for signaling the termination of the bull market in X? How much advance warning will these clues provide? For, is X apt to hover awhile before turning down, or will X reverse its course with lightning-like suddenness?

As with true love, a commodity's course seldom runs smoothly. Aside from the ever-present possibility of a sudden trend-reversal, a one-third retracement after a sizable move is not at all uncommon. If a trader fails to consider this ahead of time, such a retracement might panic him into prematurely jettisoning his position. If a trader does consider the possibility of such a retracement, he will be prepared to calmly sit it out in the event it occurs. If a trader correctly anticipates such a retracement and acts accordingly, he will either lighten up, or temporarily hedge or eliminate his entire position. Then such a retracement will simply enable him to profitably replace his prior position or further add to it with an equity undented by the retracement.

Notwithstanding his magnificent career, Ted Williams suffered many hitless days. It is no different with a highly competent commodity trader. No matter how industriously one tries to keep his eye on the ball, continuous good timing is no more humanly possible than infallibility or omniscience. Because CMA can be treacherously volatile, even a seasoned trader will from time to time find himself caught on the wrong side of the action; but one of the distinguishing characteristics of a seasoned trader is the speed with which he is able to extricate himself from a market that's going against him. Every professional risk-bearer intellectually interested in the issue is aware of a close correlation between the state of a man's psychology and the rapidity with which he is able to face and take a loss. The vital premise to be learned is: Do not persist in holding opinions that are continually being contradicted by market action. To persist in an opinion that is out of tune with reality will only further muddle your thinking. This, in turn, will deter future advantageous action-taking on your part and will, consequently, cause you to be frozen into bad positions and frozen out of good ones. An error in judgment is not cause for shame, but your stubborn defense of it can be fatal. A wrong opinion is not a disgrace, but your steadfast loyalty to it can likewise be fatal. Because markets are constantly changing, even being "right on the market" is often of but transitory benefit.

Market clues are the *only* tools that enable the assessment of market condition. But clues, to be useful, must themselves be assessed —in two principal respects:

1. Each clue must be assessed in the context of the stage through

which the market is then going. For example, a burst of volume may be bullish at one stage of market action, but bearish at another.

2. Each clue must be assessed against the entire spectrum of clues to which it is related through market action. For example, a downside breakout is a bearish clue and would, by itself, incline you to the short side of the market; but a downside breakout *from a depressed price level* (a clue) and *accompanied by a burst of volume* (another clue) should be viewed suspiciously —perhaps even as a buying opportunity.

Although all clues pointing in the same direction will comfortingly fortify your conviction, just one refutative clue may disturbingly moderate your conviction—or alter it entirely.

On the assumption that there is nothing more rewarding to the human mind than the correct solving of adequately challenging problems, you have a double incentive to unravel the mysteries of CMA. But, if you prematurely take up the commodity market challenge, your losses may very well cost you in the coin of self-respect as well as in the coin of the realm; and the commodity market, as a consequence, may permanently lose your participation. Also, if you lose money trading commodities, the only testimonial to your efforts will be the price distortions you will have created or intensified. Accordingly, this book is not a commodity market trading primer. It will not spoon-feed you from a life far removed from the Wall Street milieu to a short position in the Egg market. In a word, you would be ill-advised to tackle commodities unless or until you have successfully traded common stocks, and then you will have no further use for such a primer. Bear in mind, however, that even successful stock traders have emerged from the commodity fray with bloody noses.

Yes, there are exceptions; but those exceptional cases are almost always dictated by special circumstances. A Wheat grower who had never owned a share of common stock might, not illogically, anticipate greater profit opportunities in Wheat contracts than in stocks. A dramatic special circumstance occurred in the spring of 1967. A struggling economist, who is now an affluent consultant, was that year living in a two-room rent-controlled apartment in one of the least pretentious sections of town—and several months in arrears on his rent to boot. However, he possessed a wealth of monetary knowledge that convinced him Silver was on the threshold of a spectacular price rise. To buy Silver futures required money. To raise the money, he borrowed from friends, hocked whatever he could, and sold some family heirlooms and other personal belongings. His judgment was soon gloriously rewarded by what was undoubtedly one of the most exciting bull markets in the history of commodity trading. More to the point, our economist-turned-consultant recognized the exceptional nature of the situation that had availed him his windfall and, consequently, retired his profits from the commodity market and invested them elsewhere.

With but such rare exceptions, the profitability of your commodity trading will essentially rely on two factors:

1. Your knowledge of CMA.
2. How you apply that knowledge.

To earn profits, you need not possess the specialized knowledge of a Wheat grower or an economist. Nor need you be an active trader. In fact, even professional traders occasionally find it tactically prudent to view the action from the sidelines. Thus, by continuously following CMA whether in the fray or from the sidelines, you will significantly increase your chances of being able to benefit from those unique golden opportunities that knock on the doors of alert commodity traders with far greater than once-in-a-lifetime frequency.

According to one trading buff:
"This market's made of bullish stuff.
The shorts who've had it very rough
Will cover 'cause they've had enough.
Buy all you can, e'en on the cuff."

But claims an analytic lad,
With facts and figures on his pad:
"Demand is down, and that's real bad.
Supply is up; that's also sad.
To pay this price you must be mad."

Which leaves me where I started from;
Not very bright and feeling glum.
Perhaps it would be far less dumb
If to their brains I not succumb;
Instead let *mine* be venturesome.

4/Approaching the Action

There are two basic approaches to commodity trading:

1. Fundamental (or statistical).
2. Technical.

If there were a substantial number of *pure* fundamentalists and *pure* technicians trading commodities, it would be incumbent upon me to try to assess the merits and limitations of both approaches in painstaking detail. Happily, there are not. Most of those commodity traders who lean toward the fundamental approach concurrently keep a watchful eye on CMA, and most of those who lean toward the technical approach are mindful of the fundamentals to varying degrees. Do you remember our hero Shorty Long? Although he tried to approach Pork Bellies as a pure technician, he was still keenly aware of their "supply and demand influencing statistics." Please observe, however, that Shorty's interest in statistics confined itself almost exclusively to their effect on the market action.

The pure fundamental approach is to trade on the strength of "supply and demand influencing statistics" without giving any consideration to CMA. To so trade profitably requires a knowledge and prevision that is virtually impossible to sustain. Our economist turned consultant who made it big in Silver did so on pure fundamental factors, but he was astute enough to recognize that his good fortune could not be sustained beyond that one unusual situation. Perhaps there are some who can profit from fundamental factors alone. If so, they are essentially those professionals who devote their entire lives to the production and distribution of one or a handful of commodities.

Of all the commodities, only Gold has captivated man's imagination to a greater extent than Silver. Beginning with the early Greek and Roman civilizations, Silver has accounted for most of the world's honored coinage and a substantial portion of the assets of its more prominent national treasuries. Silver became the first monetary standard in America when the Continental Congress established the Silver dollar as a unit of value in 1776. For the past century, the price of Silver has been a principal concern of every federal administration in the United States. "The Crime of 1873" and the Bland-Allison Act, two items from our distant American past, were all about Silver. Silver cost William Jennings Bryan the Presidency. Silver legislation was a cornerstone of Franklin Roosevelt's New Deal. Today, Silver is the most popular legal currency hedge in the USA and Great Britain. India ranks as Silver's number one hoarder with Communist China probably a close second.

Ancient Greece was the world's first major Silver producer. Following the discovery of America, the Western Hemisphere took over as the world's main Silver source. Bolivia assumed the early national lead, but was quickly passed by Peru which in turn soon yielded to Mexico. Mexico held the Silver production lead from 1660 to 1871, by which time the discovery of the Comstock Lode had catapulted the USA into first place. By 1900, Mexico had regained the lead. This she has held ever since, except for 1968 when Canada temporarily surged ahead.

The USA consumes almost half the world's output of Silver. West Germany and Japan are a distant second and third in the consumption race. The photographic industry is America's number one user of Silver with the electronic and sterlingware industries running close behind in that order.

Although Hollywood has generously romanticized the mining of Silver, most Silver comes out of the ground as a by-product of Copper, Lead, and Zinc. For this reason, the production of Silver is more influenced by the prices of the other three metals than by the price of Silver itself. Silver is traded as Dust, Coin, and Bullion. Silver Coin futures are traded in New York. Silver Bullion futures are traded in New York, Chicago, Los Angeles, and London.

For centuries throughout the world, the historic monetary use of Silver has necessarily distorted the free market supply of and demand for this valued commodity. In America, the impact of this distortion finally compelled the federal government, in the 1960's, to begin withdrawing from the Silver business. The complete withdrawal was accomplished on November 11th, 1970, when the General Services Administration, with supplies exhausted, officially terminated its weekly Silver auctions. When you couple Silver's newly acquired free-market status with its characteristic role as one of man's sturdiest shields against devaluations, inflations, and other forms of statist inroads upon private property, it is no surprise that Silver is currently subject to greater fundamental scrutiny than that ever enjoyed by any other commodity. Yet, I doubt whether an FBI manhunt could have located, at any point of time since 1967, two Silver fundamentalists in close agreement over Silver's statistical position and likely resultant price course.

For over two decades, Silver consumption has been outstripping Silver production, and seems likely to continue to do so for quite some time to come. Until 1970, these deficits were met by vast government (mostly USA), industrial, and private hoards. As of 1970, the US government hoard no longer existed. Notwithstanding, Silver prices persistently declined from June of 1968 to November of 1971. Obviously, there was a time lag of unknown length between a bullish statistical situation and its translation into rising prices. (As of 1973, Silver demand had caught up with Silver's dwindling supplies with prices rising above $2.50 per ounce.) In his attempt to arrive at an answer, the pure fundamentalist must tackle many subsidiary issues. Following are some of the typical ones:

1. What is the actual Silver hoard?
2. Will world political turbulence increase, decrease, or remain about the same?
3. How will the trend of world political turbulence affect the size of the Silver hoard?
4. Will world monetary uncertainties increase, decrease, or remain about the same?
5. How will the trend of world monetary uncertainties affect the size of the Silver hoard?
6. What will be the near-term, medium-term, and long-term trends of world and US economic conditions?
7. Will Copper, Lead, and Zinc mining tend to alleviate or aggravate Silver production deficits?
8. Will technological advances enhance or diminish the industrial demand for Silver?

Let us assume that these are all the principal issues confronting a pure fundamentalist (and they certainly are not). Let us also assume a pure fundamentalist exists who is so infallible and omniscient as to in fact resolve all the subject issues with a remarkable degree of accuracy. Yet, could such a savant pinpoint the month, or even the season, when Silver prices would begin to approximately reflect Silver's shrinking supplies?

For almost 3½ years beginning June 1968, the strengthening of Silver statistics was paradoxically accompanied by a weakening of Silver prices. For the duration of this anomaly, the pure fundamentalist, blind to Silver's downward price trend, would have found no justification to enter the market except on the long side. The pure technician, on the other hand, blind to the bullish statistics, would have been able to justify only a short position. The not-so-pure fundamentalist, with an eye on the market, might very well have stayed clear of it altogether. Emotionally, he certainly could not have gone short. The not-so-pure technician, with an eye on the statistics, might have accordingly moderated his short play, prematurely closed out his short position, or been deterred from taking any short position at all. In truth, as Silver prices declined in consonance with increasingly robust fundamental factors, many "intellectual" technicians lured themselves into believing a bullish CMA existed long before it really did and were consequently prompted to buy Silver while their colleagues of the "see-no-hear-no-statistics" school were still selling it.

Fundamental factors and their assessment by others can be gleaned from a wide variety of sources. In fact, they are generally so well publicized that one, if so inclined, could become a pedestrian expert on statistics with little effort. But obtaining such material is far easier than profitably following it, because widely publicized information (including attendant opinions) is invariably discounted in the market—fully or overly. Interestingly, several schools of thought exist which advocate commodity positions that are contrary to the siren calls implied by the publicity that frequently dogs CMA. Indeed, Shorty Long will far more often buy on bad news and sell on good news than vice versa.

A join-the-crowd fundamental approach to commodity trading must result in losses. A follow-the-leader fundamental approach may result in profits if you are close enough to an astute leader. An independent fundamental approach can be of inestimable worth. The most valuable facts are those you dig up yourself and the most valuable conclusions are those at which you independently arrive. Beware, however, if the market perseveres in contradicting your fundamental assessment. In that event, the market is probably right and you wrong—at least for the time being.

Unquestionably, a foreknowledge of coming events can be a license to feather one's banking account nest. A South American dictator, about to unexpectedly confiscate his country's foreign-owned Copper properties, would do well purchasing beforehand Copper futures on the Commodity Exchange in New York or on the London Metal Exchange. A union official, knowing that an unanticipated strike against the Copper industry was incontrovertibly imminent, would do roughly as well by taking similar action. Or if a union official had advance information as to the approximate settlement date of a Copper industry strike, he would probably do quite nicely selling Copper futures before the news leaked out. In 1954, the American Army purchased a sizable quantity of Lard for consumption in West Germany. Since military purchase programs become fairly routine affairs, at least until there is a drastic numerical or logistical alteration, the Lard futures market (which, incidentally, no longer exists) reacted with predictable sophistication. What turned out not to be routine or predictable was that the Lard arrived in a totally rancid condition. The Army's impetuous reorder sent Lard prices soaring. A good whiff of that first shipment en route could have been worth the agony of an entire hitch to an enterprising G.I. Going back to the early OPA days of World War II, when price ceilings were being set on most commodities, a celebrated daughter of a celebrated VIP had no qualms about playing the commodity market on the strength of her Daddy's privileged information. Such opportunities, however, are for dreamers—not for action seekers.

There is one fundamental area with which "short-term" traders should be crucially concerned—*periodic government reports*. How short-term is "short-term"? A knotty question, but deserving of a groping answer within the framework of the following definitions:

SCALPER—a trader who intends to close out his position the same day he takes it.

SHORT-TERM TRADER—a trader who generally anticipates staying with his position for no longer than a few days, or at most roughly a week.

MEDIUM-TERM TRADER—a trader who generally anticipates staying with his position for no longer than a few weeks, or at most roughly a month.

LONG-TERM TRADER—a trader who anticipates staying with his position for at least a month.

LONG-TERM CAPITAL GAINS TRADER—a trader who seeks long-term capital gains and therefore intends to stay with his position, if profitable, for over six months.

The United States government and other governments issue a variety of periodic statistical reports covering most commodities traded as futures. These reports are released on priorly stated dates and often at specific times on those dates. The majority of these reports exercise but transitory influence on CMA; some because they are of marginal significance, and some because their results arrive as expected, thus rendering them neutral (neither bullish nor bearish). However, when an important report is not neutral, it may have a violent impact upon CMA. Consequently, unless a short-term trader is prepared to withstand the possible adverse impact of an important report or is deliberately seeking to exploit such a report, he should operate to avoid their dates of release. The release dates and market significance of government reports can be supplied by an experienced commodity broker.

Shorty Long was not only aware of a pending Pork Belly storage report, he successfully exploited it. His hope of course was that the report would be to his advantage, but this hope did not dictate his decision. What did influence Shorty's actions was his judgment that a favorable report would benefit his position to a greater extent than an unfavorable report would impair it. The lesson here is as follows:

> Subsequent to a price advance, an important bullish report is very apt to be already either partially, largely, fully, or overly discounted in the market, and any further advance sparked by such a report may thus be only minor and temporary; but a bearish report may rudely shock the market into a severe and sustained reversal. The converse would be true subsequent to a price decline. The lesson also applies to important news releases.

A fundamentalist must necessarily take government statistical reports much more seriously than a CMA follower. In fact, a fundamentalist worth his salt would be able to forecast with reasonable accuracy the contents of many of these reports. Once a report is released, the only thing left for a fundamentalist to contribute is its analysis—an analysis that will be translated into CMA long before it can be recorded and disseminated for public consumption.

Although a foreknowledge of fundamental factors can be of considerable value to its recipients, even an ordinary knowledge of plain day-to-day statistics can be comforting to a technician when such knowledge confirms and keeps on confirming his market appraisal. Yet, it's the knowledge of those technical factors which are constantly influencing CMA that is crucially essential to profitable trading on any sort of a continuing basis. A pure technical approach uses only the action of the market itself for judging the market's probable future course. The technician focuses his attention on how price is dominated by a composite estimate of current supply and demand influences in conjunction with a composite estimate of how those influences will be altered with the passage of time. In so doing, the technician may concentrate exclusively on price changes, or he may also concern himself with price changes correlated with volume, open interest, or other such factors. The clues thus generated are worthless until evaluated and translated into a judgment that triggers profitable action. Accordingly, the technician's job is to perceive as many clues as he is able, identify them as correctly as possible, and integrate them as thoroughly as he can into the entire base of his CMA knowledge. To facilitate his job, the technician usually employs some formal method of recording CMA.

I'll bet that if a chart could speak
It would most likely say:
"I think man must be quite a freak
To opt such childish play."

5/Recording the Action

If man's memory could hold an unlimited quantity of material and infallibly deliver it upon demand, the formal record-keeping of commodity price-change activity; daily high, low, and closing prices; and daily volume and open interest figures would only be required as a vehicle to facilitate the dissemination of data among those who don't already possess it. Because man's memory does not boast such qualities, and unless the filing-cabinet section of his mind is on the threshold of an evolutionary advance, ledgers, file cabinets, microfilms, charts, and the like need not fear a diminution of their utility in this respect. Indeed, even the brainiest baseball manager seems destined to keep handy a recorded reminder of his current line-up to make sure, among other things, that each of his nine players bats in proper order.

CMA followers customarily keep records. In fact, unlike baseball managers who destroy their daily line-up cards, CMA devotees frequently accumulate libraries of past records. Obviously, they must ascribe to these seemingly outdated data an important reference value. Notwithstanding, many traders do not keep such records. Floor traders, for instance, are often too embroiled in the minute-to-minute action to take time out for record-keeping. But some floor traders so treasure CMA records that they have employees assigned to their compilation and maintenance. I once witnessed with fascination a trader on the floor of the Chicago Mercantile Exchange periodically leaving the trading ring in order to scrutinize the recently recorded action of the very commodity he was professionally following. When I was introduced to him after trading hours, he told me without embarrassment that he'd feel seriously handicapped without detailed records of the immediate past within virtual elbow distance.

Boardroom scalpers, because they are generally not interested in what happened prior to the immediate past, rarely burden themselves with copious records; but many can be seen supplementing their memories by notebook pages that become increasingly jotted as trading sessions progress. Many longer-term traders do not keep CMA records for a variety of reasons. Some, not having the time or inclination, prefer either to rely on records kept by others or to subscribe to professional record-keeping services. Others disdain record-keeping as a show of mental weakness, but even they are often seen surreptitiously scrutinizing the work of colleagues. There are also those who exclusively follow the judgment of others. They, of course, have no need for records of their own. Finally, pure fundamentalists, to maintain their purity, must openly scorn CMA records. But who's to say that the files they fill, which bulge no less than the files filled by technicians, don't contain a stray chart or two?

There are, obviously, many methods of recording CMA data. Jesse Livermore, who ranks high in trading lore, was active in both stocks and commodities. Here is how he supplemented his memory in the stocks that he followed:[1]

To simplify the picture I had printed a special sheet of paper, ruled in distinctive columns, and so arranged as to give me what I term my Map for Anticipating Future Movements. For each stock I use six col-

---

[1] Jesse L. Livermore, *How to Trade in Stocks*, Investors' Press, 1966, pages 67 & 68.

umns. Prices are recorded in the columns as they occur. Each column has its heading.

> First column is headed Secondary Rally.
> Second is headed Natural Rally.
> Third is headed Upward Trend.
> Fourth is headed Downward Trend.
> Fifth is headed Natural Reaction.
> Sixth is headed Secondary Reaction.

When figures are recorded in the Upward Trend column they are entered in black ink. In the next two columns to the left I insert the figures in pencil. When figures are recorded in the Downward Trend column they are entered in red ink, and in the next two columns to the right, the entries are also made in pencil.

Although Jesse Livermore used a ledger system and others undoubtedly still do, today charts are by far the most popular record-keeping method employed by both stock market and CMA followers. They have been developed in a multitude of ways to graphically portray almost anything and everything that transpires within a trading session or over a multitude of trading sessions. The simplest type of chart would be one whereon closing prices (daily or otherwise) were plotted and connected by lines, as in Illustration III.

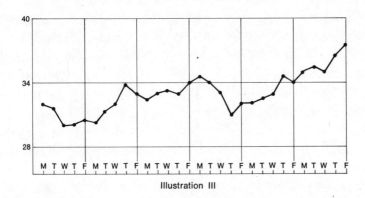

Illustration III

The chart in Illustration III is *arithmetic* as distinguished from *logarithmic*. On an arithmetic chart (Illustration IV), the numerical changes (or distances) remain constant whereas on a logarithmic chart (Illustration V), the percentage changes remain constant.

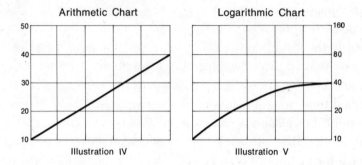

Illustration IV   Illustration V

If a CMA follower selects charts as his principal record-keeping device, he will have to resolve such basic issues as:

1. Which type of charting device should he employ?
2. Indeed, should he employ more than one charting device?
3. Should he construct his own charts; should he subscribe to a service that provides the essential charting work for him; or should he do both?

Predilection plus experience will ultimately resolve these issues for each individual. To add a word: The more you work and live with charts (self-made or purchased), the more familiar you will become with the price behavior habits of the CMA subsumed.

Before proceeding, a vital point to remember is that no matter how reliant you may become on charts, ticker tapes, or statistics, they have never done nor can ever do your thinking for you. Charts, ticker tapes, and statistics forecast nothing. Only individuals have the capacity to enjoy wisdom and vision. Charts, ticker tapes, and statistics are only tools, and tools are but aids to the formulation of sound judgment. When a fundamentalist miscalculates a supply/ demand situation, the error is his—not the statistics'. When a technician misreads the market, the error is his—not the ticker tape's. And so, when a chartist misreckons the future course of price action, the error is his—not the chart's.

In the case of arithmetic versus logarithmic charts, many common stock chart services lean to the logarithmic on the premise that this type portrays a more accurate long-term price picture. Because a commodity futures contract is relatively short-lived, arithmetic

charts should adequately serve CMA followers. With CMA followers, *vertical line charts* constructed on arithmetic chart paper are
probably the most popular. They are easy to make, easy to maintain,
and easy to read. A vertical line chart essentially represents the high,
low, and closing prices for an uninterrupted chronological series of
specified time periods—usually days. The *Commodity Research Bureau* publishes, each week, a comprehensive arithmetic vertical line
chart service that provides over 150 different charts of daily price
activity for virtually every actively traded commodity futures contract in the United States and Canada. Volume and open interest
data are also included in the chart of one futures month for all
actively traded commodities. The following, reproduced from the
Commodity Research Bureau Chart Service, is a vivid arithmetic
vertical line chart picture of Corn price action just prior to and during the the first months of the summer of 1970 Corn blight:

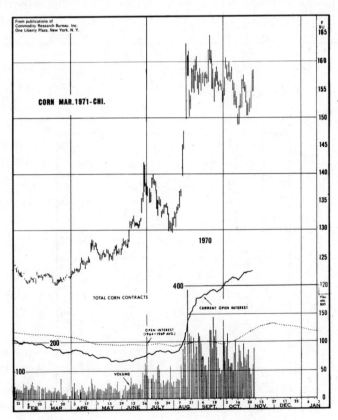

By the spring of 1971, the impact of the blight on Corn prices was visibly diminishing:

After a blight scare in June of 1972, Corn prices rapidly declined to the level from which the bull market had been launched 18 months before:

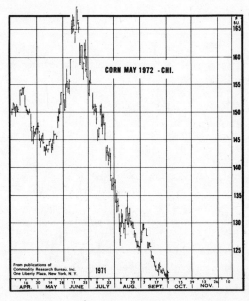

The previous charts showed daily price changes. The *Commodity Research Bureau* also issues services showing *weekly* and *monthly* price changes. Obviously, such charts can cover longer time periods. The following are examples of each, the first weekly and the second monthly:

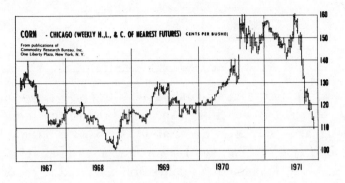

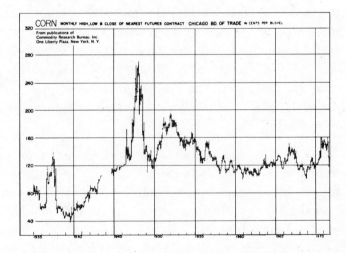

As a trading tool, daily charts are obviously much more useful than weekly or monthly ones. The principal value of weekly and monthly charts is to give a longer-term picture of a commodity's price action. A slight drawback of the longer-term charts is that they have to catenate a series of different contracts. Long-term charts of cash (or spot) prices are not handicapped by this drawback. The *Commodity Research Bureau Chart Service* includes cash-price charts for most commodities. The following is such a chart for Corn embracing the initial period of its "blight" affliction:

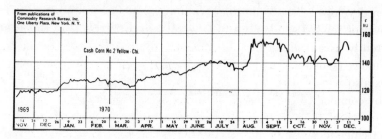

Whereas the *futures* designation applies to prices at which commodities are deliverable within a specified forward time period, the *cash* designation applies to prices at which commodities are immediately deliverable. That there is an intimate causal relationship between prices of commodities deliverable *later* and prices of those deliverable *now* is undeniable. What is subject to perennial speculation is the nature of this kinship, the tantalizing question being: Which market partner tends to dominate? Although mountainous empirical data are available, the issue remains unresolved. This would seem to testify that neither futures nor cash can be relied upon to lead the other with any profitable degree of predictability. Notwithstanding, alert CMA followers can profit from certain obvious implications:

1. If futures prices change course, the related cash price should soon follow.
2. If futures prices change course and the related cash price does not soon follow, the futures prices course change should be viewed suspiciously.
3. If a cash price changes course, the related futures prices should soon follow.
4. If a cash price changes course and the related futures prices do not soon follow, the cash price course change should be viewed suspiciously.

A very popular charting method is the *point and figure*. For those who wish to examine this method, there is no finer publication than Alexander H. Wheelan's *Study Helps in Point and Figure Tech-*

nique.[1] To quote two of Mr. Wheelan's introductory paragraphs:

Point and Figure procedure, under various names, evolved and has been developed over a long period of years and bears the stamp of approval of several generations of investors and traders. It is widely used currently as an adjunct to fundamental research by investment trusts, insurance companies, investment counselors, brokers, trust companies, etc. It is also widely used by individual investors and stock traders as well as by commodity speculators and processors.

Studies of the various fundamental factors which contribute to value are tremendously important to the professional market operator. Indeed, they are basic. But such statistical studies of securities, or of commodity economics, find it hard to measure professional and speculator psychology. This is the most unstable element in the whole array of market forces, yet it probably carries more weight in making stock or commodity prices at any given time than all the other market influences put together. Real values are not reflected in the market whenever investor and speculator confidence is lacking. In our very fast moving stock and commodity futures markets, the matter of timing is of extreme importance and it is here that technical studies, such as the Point and Figure method, will be of inestimable value. Those who have only a limited amount of time for their speculative activities in the market may entirely dispense with the fundamentals and concentrate exclusively on the technical procedure outlined herein.

Unlike the vertical line chart, a point and figure chart is not concerned with time periods. Its sole focus is on price change activity. At one extreme, such a chart may reflect but a few trading days of activity. At the other extreme, it may portray many years of CMA. Essentially, therefore, a point and figure chart is designed to represent a chronological series of *intra-day price change activity*—the activity missed by its vertical line counterpart. A widely fluctuating commodity may earn ten or twenty plots on a point and figure chart while being awarded but a single line on a vertical line chart. On the other hand, a narrowly fluctuating commodity may earn but a handful of plots on a point and figure chart while a picture of its price course may be graphically lengthening on a vertical line chart.

Graph paper is delineated by vertical lines to make columns. On

[1] Morgan, Rogers & Roberts, Inc., 150 Broadway, New York, N.Y. 10038.

a vertical line chart, as already indicated, each columnar space represents a specified time span, such as one trading day. Graph paper is also delineated by horizontal lines to make squares. On a point and figure chart, each plot in a square, usually on "X", represents a specific price change; and an advance from one column to the next denotes a price course reversal of specified magnitude. There are innumerable ways in which identical price change activity can be plotted by the point and figure method. The two basic categorical ways are: 1. *Straight price change.* 2. *Price reversal.*

On a 1¢ straight price change point and figure chart, a plot would be entered each time the price moved from one round cent to the next. Using Wheat for illustrative purposes, a move from $1.55 to $1.56 would earn the entry of one plot. A move from $1.54½ to $1.55½ would not. Although you'd be unlikely to construct a 1¢ straight chart whereon each square represented a ½ ¢ price change, on a ½ ¢ chart, each of the aforementioned moves would earn two entries. For Wheat, you could conceivably construct straight charts showing price changes of ⅛¢, ¼¢, ⅜¢, ½¢, ⅝¢ on up to any numerical denomination. Beyond 5¢, I would question the value of such a chart for Wheat. I would also question the value of more than two or three such charts for any one contract of any commodity.

Price reversal charts are constructed on the same types of graph paper as straight charts and with similar price change measuring numbers running vertically along the left-hand margin. The one difference with price reversal charts is that, before plots are entered, the price change extent must usually be at least three times greater than the vertical numerical divisions. For instance, a 3¢ reversal chart can be constructed on graph paper with price divisions of ⅛ ¢, ¼ ¢, ⅜ ¢, et cetera, but will rarely be constructed on graphs where the price division is over 1¢.

Still using Wheat as our illustration, let's consider two 3¢ reversal charts, one on graph paper with ½ ¢ divisions and the other on graph paper with 1¢ divisions. After Wheat declines from $1.59 to $1.55½, it reverses and goes back up to $1.58½. The decline is plotted in column 1. In column 2 on the ½ ¢ chart, six new plots are entered; but in column 2 on the 1¢ chart, no new plots are entered. However, had the price gone back up to $1.59, seven new plots would be entered on the ½ ¢ chart and three new plots would be entered on the 1¢ chart. Once $1.59 is reached, each additional ½¢ advance earns a plot on the ½¢ chart and each additional 1¢ advance earns a plot on the 1¢ chart. Although the restrictions are more severe for plotting price change activity on reversal charts than on straight ones, reversal charts can be constructed in a greater variety of ways. Six conventional type charts (Illustration VI) constructed from the following price change activity should further clarify point and figure procedural methods:

20½, 21, 20¾, 21½, 21¼, 21¾, 21½, 22, 21¾, 22, 21½, 21¾, 21¼, 21¾, 21½, 22, 21¼, 21½, 20¾, 21¼, 21, 21½, 21¼, 22, 21¼, 21¾, 21, 21¼, 20¾, 21, 20¾, 21, 20½, 21, 20¾, 21¼, 21, 21¾, 21½, 22¼, 22, 22½, 22, 22½, 22¼, 23, 22¾, 23½, 23¼, 23¾, 23¼, 23½, 23, 23½, 22¾, 23, 22¼, 22¾, 22½, 23, 22¼, 22½, 21¾, 22, 21½, 22, 21¾, 22¼, 22, 22¼, 22, 22½, 21¾, 22, 21¼, 21½, 21, 21¼, 20¾, 21½, 21¼, 21¾, 21½, 22, 21¼, 21½, 21, 21¾, 21½, 22¼, 22, 22½, 22¼, 23, 22, 22¼, 21½.

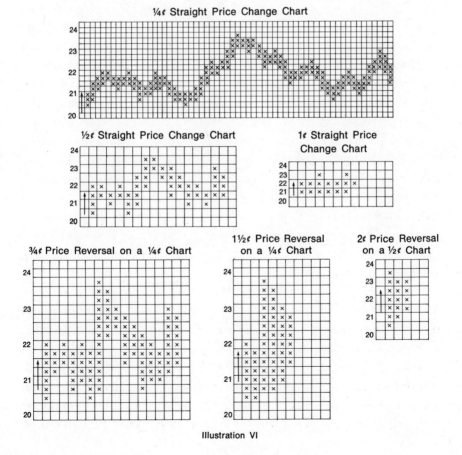

Illustration VI

The preceding price change activity might have taken place within a day, week, month, or over a longer period of time. The time span which covers a specific range of price change activity largely dictates the price change magnitude practical for plotting. If activity such as the foregoing customarily occurs within a single day for a particular commodity, plotting ¼ ¢ price changes might soon overwhelm one with bulging chart facilities.

Each man on earth who works and strives
Would benefit from double lives.
With first for practice, error, trial;
The next would be a constant smile.

6/Certain Action Considerations of 21 Commodities

As indicated in Chapter 3, a clue by itself—isolated from all others—has little or no market forecasting significance. A burst of volume can be one of the most helpful clues in assessing CMA, but its insulation from other evidential material renders it valueless except as a suggestion that meaningful action is probably taking place. Also, what may be meaningful to Copper might be less meaningful, or not meaningful at all, to Eggs; what may have applied to Cotton in 1962 might not apply to Cotton in 1972; or what may apply to February Pork Bellies might not apply to August Pork Bellies.

In every respect, each commodity enjoys some unique characteristics, and each commodity shares some of the same characteristics with certain other commodities. In the realm of news items and developments, a Carribbean hurricane might perk up Orange Juice prices, but will probably not affect any other commodities traded as futures. On the other hand, a threatened drought in the Midwest will not only stimulate all American grain prices, but will even have a derivative effect on Canadian grain prices.

As to factors of a purer fundamental nature, adverse business conditions will lessen the demand for Copper and Silver, but will increase the demand for Eggs and Potatoes. An increase in American tariffs, import duties, or other "restraint-of-trade" measures will lessen the demand for Cotton, Soybean Oil, and all those other farm products we export on balance. Correspondingly, such measures will impair American demand for Sugar and Cocoa, products we import on balance, to the extent these measures pertain to them.

A *seasoned* commodity is said to be one whose contracts have been trading for a long time, perhaps a quarter of a century or more. A *liquid* commodity is said to be one whose contracts enjoy a large following by speculators and by such professional tradesmen as manufacturers, merchants, processors, warehousemen, and the like. A seasoned commodity is not necessarily a liquid one, and vice versa.

Most technical clues vary in conclusiveness with the degree of seasoning or liquidity enjoyed by the commodity in question. For instance, a congestion area breakout is more likely to be valid with seasoned and liquid commodities whereas volume bursts are more likely to be meaningful with unseasoned and semiliquid ones. On the other hand, the validity of gap action clues is ordinarily divorced from seasoning or liquidity considerations. Most importantly, each commodity's endowments are in a constant state of flux. Therefore, observation and experience translated into a growing knowledge must predominate the salient but changing characteristics that are outlined in the next part of this chapter:

> 1. Money and cash were once said to be dough,
> But now they are labeled just bread.
> Why not go back to their causative mow
> By using the WHEAT term instead?

Wheat is one of the most seasoned and liquid of all the commodities. Among the grains, it is usually second only to Soybeans in price volatility. Because Wheat in most years has enjoyed at least two medium-term or long-term moves of from 10¢ to 25¢, this commodity is especially appealing to medium-term and long-term traders. Its high liquidity, moreover, makes it virtually as appealing to scalpers. But Wheat has been a chronic disappointment to long-term capital gains seekers. Except during major wars, the bear side of Wheat has been far more lucrative than the bull side. After reaching $3.20 a bushel in the late 1940's, Wheat embarked upon a two-decade bear market that saw it dip below $1.20 in 1968. Wheat is a *crop-year* commodity with each new year for traders beginning with the July contract. Old crop-year Wheat, however, can be stored for a considerable length of time, rendering carry-over supplies an important price consideration.

Wheat is priced in dollars and cents per bushel with a contract containing 5,000 bushels.

> 2. CORN can be used in many ways.
> It's even used in alcohol.
> The farmer says it often pays
> To feed his livestock with it all.

Corn, generally, is as seasoned and liquid as Wheat, but less volatile. Although more often than not a relatively unexciting market performer, Corn's huge speculative following indicates that many traders prefer its milder-paced action. Like Wheat, Corn went into a bear market spin in the late 1940's, declining from $2.70 a bushel to around $1.00 in 1960, and hitting $1.00 again in 1968. Corn has roughly the same carry-over considerations as Wheat, but its crop-year usually begins with the December contract. An early harvest can bring in some new-crop Corn in time for the September contract. Whereas Wheat is one of man's more important food products, Corn is the farm animal's principal feed. As such, high Corn prices render it especially vulnerable to substitute or competing products.

Corn is priced in dollars and cents per bushel with a contract containing 5,000 bushels.

> 3. Though OATS, like snails, are very slow,
> They're faster than most stocks I know.

Oats are very seasoned, fairly liquid, and one of the least volatile of all the commodities. Since 1952, this grain has been ambling between 55¢ and 85¢ per bushel. It has the same crop-year as Wheat and excess supplies can be held in storage. Like Corn, Oats are largely used as a farm animal feed. Consequently, Oat prices tend to tag after Corn prices.

Oats are priced in dollars and cents per bushel with a contract containing 5,000 bushels.

> 4. The SOYBEAN has so much real zing.
> Alive, it sure could boast one thing:
> A sex life any human being
> Would love to own for just next Spring.

The Soybean, though actually an oilseed, is regarded as a grain. Since World War II, this commodity has consistently ranked near the top in popularity as a trading vehicle. Its high volatility has made it a technician's darling and its uniquely intricate statistical situation has established it as a fundamentalist's delight. Except for seed and occasional feed, almost all this crop is crushed to obtain oil and meal. Thus is formed a complex whose components not only importantly influence each other pricewise, but are also importantly influenced by foreign Soybean products as well as by dozens of other competing products engendered both at home and abroad. For the past quarter of a century (until 1973), Soybeans had fluctuated between $2.10 and $4.40 per bushel. Although the Soybean, like most other commodities traded as futures, has experienced extended periods of price inactivity, since World War II it has averaged better than one 50¢ move per year. A key reason for the Soybean's price volatility is that the broad commercial use of its by-products has kept carry-over supplies from becoming a market depressant. Soybean's one drawback as a trading vehicle is that its bull markets are noted for their unexpected and sudden collapses. The Soybean crop-year begins with the September contract, but late August rains can delay the harvest. In the September Soybean contract, therefore, even the anticipation of the possibility of such an occurrence can trigger eye-bulging action.

Soybeans are priced in dollars and cents per bushel with a contract containing 5,000 bushels.

5. Our SOYBEAN OIL's in good demand
   In almost every foreign land.
   This helps the purposeful crusade
   To further broaden world-wide trade.

Soybean Oil, the second component of the Soybean complex, is the world's most widely used edible vegetable oil. Soybean Oil is a relative newcomer to futures trading, having been launched on the Chicago Board of Trade in 1950. Notwithstanding, it enjoys a high degree of liquidity. The Korean War promptly sent its price up to 22¢ per pound. Since then, it has ranged mostly between 7¢ and 14¢. Although not quite as volatile as its Soybean parent, Soybean Oil is a better vehicle for the long-term and maxi-term bullishly inclined trader. Oil is storable and its production-year begins with the October contract.

Soybean Oil is priced in cents per pound with a contract containing 60,000 pounds.

6. Domestic fowl are said to wish
   For SOYBEAN MEAL as their main dish.

Soybean Meal, the third component of the Soybean complex, is mostly fed to livestock. It began trading on the Chicago Board of Trade in 1951, is only moderately liquid, and, in refutation of its perishability, is not nearly as volatile as the other two members of its appellative family. Since the inception of its futures contracts and until the fall of 1972, Meal had roamed between $45 and $110 per ton. Its main interest is to straddlers of the Soybean complex components. Meal's production-year begins with the October contract.

Soybean Meal is priced in dollars and cents per ton with a contract containing 100 tons.

In commodity jargon, a *perishable* crop or product is one that cannot be stored from one crop-year or production-year to the next. Of the twenty-one commodities covered in this chapter, only four are perishable by this definition: Soybean Meal, Potatoes, Eggs, and Pork Bellies. Although Soybean Oil is far more perishable than

Copper, it is still not technically considered perishable. All things being equal, one would expect perishable items to be more volatile pricewise than nonperishable ones. Of the perishable items, as may be gathered from the previous paragraph, Soybean Meal is the notable exception. The reason is that its price is constantly being hemmed in by competing animal feeds. When supplies shorten and Meal prices concomitantly rise, other feeds are quickly substituted. When supplies grow increasingly abundant and prices concomitantly fall, Meal is quickly sought as a substitute for other feeds. As for nonperishable items, large carry-over supplies, when they exist, act as a severe price depressant. This in turn subdues volatility. Albeit, when carry-over supplies are either non-burdensome or nonexistent, nonperishable commodities are as qualified as perishable ones to participate in the volatility sweepstakes.

> 7. I'd even hate done to a bird
> The very nasty deed
> Suggested by that silly word
> Which names the crop RAPESEED.

Rapeseed, traded on the Winnipeg Grain Exchange, has recently captured the fascination of many CMA followers. Although around only since 1963 and not nearly as liquid as domestic grains, Rapeseed's customary high volatility should ensure its ultimate success as a trading vehicle. Already it's an ideal medium for scalpers as intra-day moves of 3¢ and higher are more the rule than the exception. In its brief hectic history, and except for February and March 1973, Rapeseed has raced back and forth within $2.00 and $3.80 per bushel. The crop-year of this storable grain begins with the November contract.

Rapeseed is priced in dollars and cents per bushel with a contract containing 5,000 bushels.

> 8. Good COCOA may be quite a treat
> For people of all ages.
> But Cocoa's often not as sweet
> To its staunch market sages.

Cocoa is entirely foreign grown. It's been traded in New York and London for many years and has usually boasted a strong commercial and speculative following. Its range since the Korean War has been 15¢ to 45¢ per pound except in 1954 when it soared to 65¢ and 1965 when it plunged to 10¢. Cocoa is a storable crop, but carry-over supplies did not become a problem until roughly 1960. Consequently, Cocoa was much more volatile in the 1950's than it has been in the past dozen years. In addition to the moderation of its fluctuations, high brokerage commission rates make this commodity unappealing to the scalper and short-term trader. Also, frequent political invasion of the Cocoa market constitutes an annoying and tricky obstacle for the fundamental analyst. Cocoa's crop-year begins with the December contract.

Cocoa is priced in cents per pound with a contract containing 30,000 pounds.

> 9. When Castro's face is in a frown,
> Could be his SUGAR crop is down.

Sugar is mostly grown abroad. That which is grown in the States is not nearly enough to satisfy domestic needs. Like Cocoa, Sugar has been traded in New York and London for many years; but Sugar, in recent years, has boasted a much stronger following than its sweet-tooth rival. *World* Sugar, as distinguished from the non-liquid *domestic* Sugar, has enjoyed a spectacular market history since World War II. The Korean War sent it up to 8¢ per pound from where it promptly tumbled to less than 4¢. Then, in one month, from December 1957 to January 1958, it more than doubled. By the end of 1958, however, it was back to where it had started. Next came Castro, and Sugar soared to over 13¢, fell back down to 4½¢, and then recovered to 12¢—all in 1963. Three years later it was mired under 2¢, suddenly more than doubled, just as suddenly fell back below 2¢, doubled again, and after that slowly retreated to 1½¢ where it languished in the fall of 1968. But Sugar wasn't destined to languish for long. With little delay it embarked upon a bull market which was to roar for over three years. Frequent depressed Sugar prices in the past have been caused by burdensome carry-over supplies stemming from ill-advised producer exuberance. Because Sugar is continuously being planted or harvested somewhere in the world, crop-year considerations are of but minor significance.

Sugar is priced in dollars and cents per pound with a contract containing 112,000 pounds.

10. I say this as a breakfast fan:
Fresh ORANGE JUICE is better than
The stuff committed to the can.

Orange Juice is one of the younger commodities and, consequently, is not yet endowed with more than a moderate degree of
liquidity. Nonetheless, it has experienced a highly volatile market
history since its introduction to CMA followers in 1966. From 29¢
per pound, it vaulted to 75¢ in 1968. It then steadily retreated to
32¢ in January 1971, but by November of that year it had rallied
back to 65¢. Orange Juice prices are uniquely sensitive to certain
weather developments or their threats, such as hurricanes and
freezes. The price convulsions thereby generated have given many
nightmares to this commodity's followers. Although Orange Juice
is storable, each new crop-year, which begins with the January contract, usually launches a completely new ball game.

Orange Juice is priced in cents per pound with a contract containing 15,000 pounds.

11. *Potatoes* of Maine, you ought to know,
Do differ from those of Idaho.

Although Potatoes are grown in most states, the Maine crop is by
far the largest. Maine Potato contracts have been traded on the New
York Mercantile Exchange since 1941. Idaho Potato contracts have
been traded on the Chicago Mercantile Exchange only since 1968.
This highly perishable crop begins its year in New York with the
November contract. The May contract, however, is the one on which
most interest is focused. In response to this single contract interest,
Idaho Potatoes only offer a May contract. The New York May contract is more liquid than the one in Chicago, but the latter is gradually catching up. As the winter months progress, both May contracts,
empirically, can be expected to increase in volatility. Thus, for about
three months of most years, these contracts are ideal for the scalper,
mini-term, and short-term trader. Also, the nominal margin requirements per contract make this commodity an excellent trading vehicle
for action seekers with modest bankrolls. Potatoes are almost as sensitive to weather news as Orange Juice; but the Potato cash market,
by reason of its being so much more seasoned than the Orange Juice

cash market, receives weather scares with greater sophistication. Maine Potatoes have thrice risen above $6.00 per hundredweight. In years when abundant crops have been accompanied by good weather conditions, Maine Potato prices have customarily slid beneath $2.00. Until 1973, the better quality Idaho Potatoes ranged between $4.00 and $7.50.

Potatoes are priced in cents per pound (or in dollars and cents per hundredweight) with a contract containing 50,000 pounds.

As this is being written, there is a bill before Congress to ban trading in Potato futures. There is precedent for passage of this bill. In 1958, a bill was passed to ban trading in Onion futures.

By the time this book is published, the subject bill may have been passed. Hopefully, it will never be passed. The arguments against the bill could fill a tome. The arguments in favor of the bill are totally specious. Those who fought to ban trading in Onion futures were mostly owners of large Onion farms. Those who are fighting to ban trading in Potato futures are mostly owners of large Potato farms. Their very opposition to futures markets in their crops is magnificent testimony to the productivity of such markets.

Why should any growers wish to destroy their crops' futures markets? There can be but one answer: Without these markets, growers can charge the consumer higher prices. Why? Because, without these markets, there is no valid daily price advertising to aid efficient purchasing.

In the ten years preceding the Onion futures ban (1949-1958), the average price in dollars per CWT. received by Onion growers throughout the United States was $2.75. For Potatoes during the same ten years, the average price in dollars per hundredweight was $2.00. The corresponding figure for Onions during the ten-year period 1961-1970 was $3.84, and for Potatoes $2.06. The overall increase in Onion prices was just shy of 40% whereas the overall increase in Potato prices was a bare 3%. When growers get more, consumers pay more. Ralph Nader take note.

Since this thesis does not fill a tome, it is necessarily an oversimplification which leaves countless questions unanswered. The point, however, has been implicitly made, to wit: If you are a price-conscious consumer, protect and encourage the growth of free markets everywhere; including, naturally, the commodity futures markets.

> 12. Cool air-conditioning's good for man
>   In any tepid clime.
>   It shortens, too, the laying span
>   Of hens in summertime.
>   This means more EGGS for us to eat,
>   And cheaper Eggs as well.
>   It also means we need less meat
>   To keep us feeling well.

Eggs, though traded by generations of CMA followers, have only succeeded in achieving a moderate degree of liquidity. This product's high perishability and other features have not only rendered its market action one of the most volatile around, but have also on occasion caused its price behavior to be downright disorderly. In attempts to eliminate this market's disorderliness, the contracts have been changed from time to time to the point where they are now closely related to the cash market. In so doing, production-year considerations have also been virtually eliminated. Since World War II, Eggs have fluctuated between 20¢ and 65¢ per dozen. Because 10¢ to 20¢ swings within a period of one or two months are frequent occurrences, this commodity serves as a fine trading vehicle for scalpers, short-term traders, and medium-term traders with strong stomachs and nerves of steel.

Eggs are priced in cents per dozen with a contract containing 22,500 dozen.

> 13. BELLIES are fun because they move fast.
>   Sleep at the switch and wake up aghast.

Pork Bellies unobtrusively appeared on stage in 1961. Before 1965 was out, however, this commodity had attained stardom. Though never quite achieving the liquidity of such superstars as Soybeans and Sugar, the day-to-day, even hour-to-hour, volatility of this product has frequently had CMA followers throughout the country diverted from their other pursuits during Pork Bellies' 3½ hours of trading action. In 1966, this action had become so exhausting to the brokers on the floor of the Chicago Mercantile Exchange that daily trading was for a while reduced by an hour. Highly perishable, the Pork Belly year begins with the February contract. Its final August contract can be unusually acrobatic if supplies become either unexpectedly tight or unexpectedly burdensome. From just over 20¢ per pound in 1964, Bellies rose to over 55¢ by December 1965. 1968 saw Bellies again under 25¢, but by 1970, they had recovered to 48¢. A bear market then plunged them to 27¢ from where they smartly recovered without too much delay. Many traders judge Pork Belly congestion area action to be potentially more lucrative than Pork Belly trend action.

Pork Bellies are priced in cents per pound with a contract containing 36,000 pounds.

> 14. When Corn is dear, a farmer won't
> Long keep his HOGS from slaughter;
> But when Corn's cheap, he shelters them
> More even than his daughter.

Hogs, of which Pork Bellies are a part, owe their growing popularity as a speculative medium to the popularity of their bacon by-product. Trading in Hog futures began in 1966. Until the fall of 1972, prices had ranged between 16¢ and 30¢ per pound. There is, understandably, a strong correlation between Hog and Pork Belly prices.

Hogs are priced in cents per pound with a contract containing 30,000 pounds.

> 15. The West was won by brave men who
> Faced every sort of battle.
> Among them were the ones who strived
> To grow the nation's CATTLE.

Cattle futures made their debut in 1964. The contracts enjoyed but limited speculative appeal until 1969 when Cattle experienced its first bull market. After intermediate declines, Cattle prices rose again in both 1970 and 1971. This recent volatility has increased Cattle's liquidity and thereby promoted it to number two in popularity among the meat products traded as futures. Prior to 1972,

Cattle had ranged from 24¢ to 36¢ per pound. It is not yet as satisfactory a vehicle for scalpers and short-term traders as it is for traders who incline toward the longer view. Because the Cattle contract calls for delivery of live steers, Cattle is not technically a perishable commodity; nor does it lend itself to significant product-year considerations.

Cattle is priced in cents per pound with a contract containing 40,000 pounds.

> 16. There was a time when COTTON reigned
>   As king of all our crops.
>   Its recent comeback in world trade
>   Returns it 'mongst the tops.

After being the darling of CMA followers since virtually the birth of this nation, Cotton fell prey to political invasion in 1953. Lured by the emergence of a new contract in 1967 and tantalized by galvanic bull markets in 1967 and 1971, a new generation of subjects is fast returning the former king of American crops to its rightful status. Although the most seasoned commodity of them all, Cotton hasn't yet fully regained its lost liquidity. Notwithstanding, it is an excellent vehicle for all trader categories. Since the 1967 contract change, Cotton has ranged between 24¢ and 44¢ per pound. This storable crop begins its year with the October contract.

Cotton is priced in cents per pound with a contract containing 50,000 pounds.

> 17. Our COPPER cent of all our coins
>   Alone has stood time's test.
>   Then why does it not even draw
>   A beggar's shy request?

Copper, traded for generations in both New York and London, is supposed to have been the first metal used by man for other than ornamentation. Alloyed with Tin, Copper made possible the Bronze Age. Pricewise, this commodity is a mover—rarely remaining in a congestion area for long periods of time. Beginning with January 1964, it rose from 30¢ per pound to 60¢, declined to 38¢, rose to over 80¢, declined to 46¢, rose again to 60¢, declined to 42¢, rose to 76¢, declined to 44¢, rose to 78¢, fell back to 45¢, rallied to 58¢, and then sunk to under 45¢. Its 1973 bull market rallied it to over 60¢. Copper's high volatility and good liquidity make it an excellent medium for quick trades while its hitherto periodic bull moves suggest it as an excellent potential vehicle for the long-term capital gains seeker. All metal and wood products are storable and consequently entail no significant production-year considerations.

Copper is priced in cents per pound with a contract containing 25,000 pounds.

18. SILVER and the trial of Scopes
Dashed Will Bryan's fondest hopes.

Silver, after erupting in 1967 from its fixed price of approximately $1.29 per troy ounce, traveled a dramatic journey during which it built up a huge speculative and commercial following. It climaxed near $2.60 in 1968, and then proceeded upon a Napoleonic retreat that ultimately sent it all the way back to its initial point of departure. Silver is not only highly popular with traders of every category, it has also become *the* most popular vehicle for tax straddling. As a consequence, volume action in Silver must be appraised with this in mind.

Silver is priced in dollars and cents per troy ounce with a New York contract containing 10,000 troy ounces and a Chicago contract containing 5,000 troy ounces.

19. The Puerto Ricans make our rum.
The Russians mine most PLATINUM.

More than half the world's Platinum is produced in Russia. For that reason, this is one commodity fundamentalists would be well-advised to avoid. Historically a dull commodity, Platinum first attracted attention by following the 1967-1968 Silver bull market, rising from $160 to $300 per troy ounce. During Silver's retreat, Platinum was an equally loyal and dogged camp follower. At the point of departure, however, Platinum failed to halt. Instead, it retreated so much farther that, on two occasions, it actually dipped below $100. Thanks to anti-pollutionists, Platinum prices are currently (1973) on the rise. As a semiliquid commodity, Platinum's principal appeal would seem to be to the seeker of long-term capital gains.

Platinum is priced in dollars and cents per troy ounce with a contract containing 50 troy ounces.

> 20. PLYWOOD spawned a Dali fan.
> It also spawned a Congress man.

Plywood contracts have been traded only since 1969, but it can already boast high volatility and rapidly increasing liquidity. Prior to 1972, its price had ranged from $65 to $110 per 1,000 square feet. Rapidly changing supply and demand considerations for this product strongly indicate that it will soon join the leaders in the futures popularity parade.

Plywood is priced in dollars and cents per square foot with a contract containing 69,120 square feet.

> 21. The LUMBER market should be good;
> It's still in infancy.
> It will be fun to watch this wood
> From here to puberty.

Lumber, like Plywood, is also a newcomer to CMA followers. Understandably, its price range and action have roughly paralleled Plywood's. Lumber has not as yet attracted the following enjoyed by Plywood, but its volatile nature should not go long unnoticed.

Lumber is priced in dollars and cents per board foot with a contract containing 100,000 board feet.

Cocoa, Copper, Silver, and Sugar are actively traded both in New York and in London. While awaiting the opening of New York's markets, traders study news tickers in the knowledge that London's action will affect New York's opening prices. Concomitantly, New York's action will affect London's opening prices on the following business day. The same unresolved issue applies here as it does to futures and cash prices (briefly discussed in Chapter 6), the subject issue being: "Which market partner tends to dominate?" The answer here is the same: namely, "The issue remains unresolved."

Cash prices of most commodities other than metals and woods have marked seasonal variations. In broad general terms, this means that the cash price of a crop tends to be cheapest during harvest season, tends to rise thereafter until some point of time prior to the next harvest, and then tends to decline as the new harvest approaches. Cash prices of such products as Pork Bellies also have marked seasonal variations, Bellies tending to be cheapest a few months after the peak Hog slaughter. Most fundamentalists claim that cash price seasonal variations carry over to the futures markets and accordingly publicize these seasonals so widely that it is more difficult to avoid the information than to come by it. This information is of such dubious value that I recommend its avoidance for the following principal reasons:

1. With respect to most commodities, for instance the grains, no two fundamentalists seem to agree what the seasonal price variations precisely are. The answer here is simply that the posture of these seasonals is tenuous and transitory—being incontrovertibly altered from year to year.

2. With those commodities that have fairly immutable seasonal price variations,, like Potatoes, the futures markets fully discount them. For example, Maine Potatoes habitually sell for about $1.00 per pound less in the fall than in the spring. Thus, the New York November contract customarily begins trading at around $2.50 and the May contract at around $3.50. Since the November contract cannot be stored over the winter months and since the anticipated Potato cash price rise is already fully reflected in the May contract, what profit can there be in the knowledge of this particular seasonal?

3. Even assuming that futures prices can be affected by cash price seasonal variations, this knowledge is so extensively broadcasted that its usefulness would seem virtually demolished by the very publicity that attends it.

The various contract months representing a particular commodity almost always trade at differing prices. These price differentials reflect many factors of which seasonal variation is but one. To discount factors that are likely to affect forward prices is one of the many contributions made by the futures markets. To discount seasonal price variations is a contribution the futures markets have no difficulty in making. Consequently, detailed seasonal data were not included in the foregoing 21-commodity review.

Another area not included in the review was how government price-controlling measures have influenced, do influence, or may subsequently influence futures prices. The reason is that the limited knowledge acquired from any presentation short of a comprehensive exposition could be far more dangerous than valuable. A case in point is the grain price declines that followed the Korean War. The hope that grains would stop declining at government "support levels" prompted many traders to buy grains at these levels in the belief that they had much more to gain than to lose. Dismayingly, grain prices plunged through the support levels in total disregard of their existence. The lesson here is: When the market does battle with government policy, place your bets on the market.

One topic that was featured is liquidity. To further stress the importance of liquidity, the following is part of what I wrote on the subject in 1961:

Liquidity is the most overlooked attribute of the market place. Where liquidity is present to a large degree, buyers and sellers do not materially suffer from the price differentials between the bid prices and the asked prices, and trade is accordingly brisk. Where liquidity is largely absent, buyers and sellers suffer from the price spreads, and trade is accordingly dull. The second-hand automobile market is quite liquid. Car owners of even modest means can enjoy the luxury of periodic taste changes. The second-hand furniture market lacks liquidity. Only the wealthy can afford the luxury of periodic furniture taste changes.

Also:

Ultimately, liquidity is made possible by traders, speculators, scalpers, or whatever you wish to term them. A trader makes profits by correcting price distortions. The profits a trader makes precisely match the quantitative extent of the net distortions he corrects. The more successful a trader is, the more future liquidity he will be able to provide for the markets in which he functions.

However commendable it may be to provide liquidity for a market, that is not a trader's job; it is merely a consequence of his job

Anthony M. Reinach, *The Nature of Puts & Calls*, The Bookmailer, 1961, pages 25 & 26.

when properly performed over an extended period of time. Therefore, a trader should stick to markets that are either already liquid or are gaining liquidity, and should avoid non-liquid markets or markets that are losing liquidity. Except for Idaho Potatoes, all commodity futures offer multiple months in which to trade contracts. Traders should select the most liquid contract months that meet with their objectives. The cash month, the current calendric one, often becomes extremely volatile. Do not be lured by this volatility into trading a cash month. Indeed, a trader should not even hold a position into this month. In the first place, the liquidity of a cash month contract, by its very nature, is being rapidly wound down. Secondly, holding a cash month contract exposes one to the threat of demand for obligatory fulfillment.

The liquidity of a commodity will often determine how a trader chooses to execute an order. Following are the principal methods of executing orders:

1. MARKET—A *market* order must be executed immediately by the floor broker at the most favorable price possible. A market order in semiliquid commodities is ill-advised except when a trader is in a hurry to take or dispose of a position, and even then the trader might improve his execution by parceling out his order a few contracts at a time spaced five or ten minutes apart.

2. NOT HELD or TAKE YOUR TIME—A *not held* or *take your time* order is always used in conjunction with a market order and simply constitutes an added instruction to the floor broker to inject his personal judgment in timing the execution on the implied condition that he will not be held accountable should his judgment turn out questionable. The objective, of course, is to achieve an execution better than that which would have been achieved by a pure market order. Such an order, however, is usually advisable only when the trader or his account executive knows the floor broker handling the order, *and* vice versa.

3. LIMIT—A *limit* order constitutes an instruction to the floor broker not to buy above or sell below a specified price. If May Pork Bellies were trading at 36.20, a trader wishing to purchase 10 contracts on a dip might enter a buy order with a limit of 35.95 or, merely, a buy limit order at 35.95. If he wanted to

purchase those contracts at or near the then current market, he might enter a buy limit order at 36.20 or 36.25 in the knowledge a market order could find him paying 36.30 or 36.35 for that which he might well have purchased 5 to 15 points cheaper. Needless to say, he could fail to acquire the desired position, partially or altogether, in either of the two foregoing events. A buy limit order is customarily placed near or below the market and a sell limit order near or above the market. A limit order can be used to take or dispose of a position and can be entered for a period of time from fill-or-kill to as long as the contract in question is scheduled to exist.

4. FILL-OR-KILL—A *fill-or-kill* order is always used in conjunction with a limit order placed near the market and is essentially a technique designed to complete a multiple contract order all at once or not at all. A trader enters a fill-or-kill order to buy 10 May Bellies at 36.25 when Bellies are trading in that vicinity. Several things could be in the trader's mind. For one, the trader might not want to get involved for just two or three contracts. For another, the trader might figure, if seven or eight contracts are readily available at his price, the floor broker will make a special effort to get him supplied with the remainder so that the entire order will not be lost.

5. SCALE—A *scale* order is a limit order used to establish or liquidate a position as a market moves down or up. Wishing to buy 20 May Bellies if the market sells off from 36.25, a trader might enter four 5-contract buy orders at 36.15, 36.10, 36.05, and 36.00. Conversely, wishing to sell May Bellies if the market rises from 36.25, a trader might enter four 5-contract sell orders at 36.35, 36.40, 36.45, and 36.50.

6. STOP—A *stop* order is similar to a limit order but differs from it in three respects. First, whereas a limit order is often placed near the market, a stop order is practically never so placed. Second, whereas a buy limit order is always placed below the market when not placed near it, a buy stop order is always placed above the market. The opposite is true with a sell limit order and a sell stop order. Third, whereas a limit order can be executed only at the specified price or better and might never be executed even though the specified price is ticked, a stop

order is automatically executed as a market order immediately when the specified price is ticked.

7. STOP LIMIT—A *stop limit* order is a stop order with the added stipulation that the floor broker may not execute it beyond a specified price. For example, a trader enters a buy Stop order for 10 May Bellies at 36.55 with a limit of 36.60. This means that, when May Bellies tick 36.55, the order automatically becomes one to buy 10 May Bellies at 36.60 or better. Like a limit order, a stop limit order may go permanently unexecuted.

8. MARKET-IF-TOUCHED (MIT)—An *MIT* order is a buy order below the market or a sell order above the market that becomes a stop order the moment the specified price is ticked.

9. CONTINGENT—A *contingent* order is either a stop or an MIT order that is executed in one contract upon the ticking of a specified price in another contract.

How many commodities should one follow? That depends upon how much time one has to devote to the futures markets. It also depends upon many other considerations that can only be individually determined. One obvious axiom does apply: The more commodities one follows, the more profit opportunities he will encounter. Conversely, the fewer commodities one follows, the more familiar he will become with his selections. Some traders claim they owe their success to being constantly on top of a dozen or more commodities; and other traders claim they owe their success to knowing just one, two, or three commodities as intimately as they know their own bedrooms.

The twenty-one commodities briefly reviewed in this chapter were, of course, arbitrarily chosen. They are the ones that currently seem most qualified to meet all conventional trading objectives. Such a list probably would not have been the same a year ago, and probably will not be the same a year from now. Also, such a list compiled by another probably would not be identical to the subject one. However, since so very few CMA followers interest themselves in as many as twenty-one commodities, this list should be eminently serviceable—for it includes all the habitual action-packed items in the futures markets.

It's said that Bulls and Bears make dough
But Pigs just never do;
Yet who will tell us where to draw
The line between the two?
They also say to buy when weak
And sell on shows of strength.
Again, who'll tell us how to gauge
An action's likely length?

7/Basic Types of Action

Broadly speaking, CMA may be divided into two basic categories:

1. Trend.
2. Congestion Area.

Illustration VII is an over-simplified example of trend action punctuated by congestion area action.

On a price chart, a *trend* may be considered to exist between any two points on essentially different planes. In Illustration VII, BC, DE, FG, and HI are all trends. A trend may also be considered to exist between any two points on essentially different planes even when interrupted by one or more congestion areas, such as between 'A' and 'F', between 'B', and 'H', or between 'E' and 'I'. Concomitantly, a *congestion area* may be considered to exist between any two points on an essentially similar plane. In the foregoing illustration, AB, CD, EF, and GH are all congestion areas. A congestion area may also be considered to exist between any two points on an

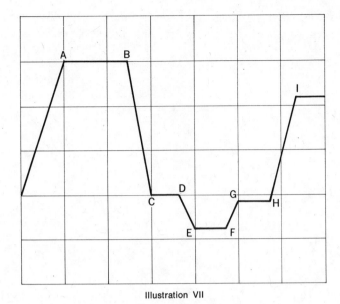

Illustration VII

essentially similar plane even when interrupted by two or more trends, such as between 'C' and 'H'.

Direction is the initial way of identifying *trends*. Hence, BC and DE are *down*trends (as are also the overall actions between 'A' and 'F' and between 'B' and 'H') while FG and HI are *up*trends (as is also the overall action between 'E' and 'I'). Location in the price history portrayed is the initial way of identifying congestion areas. Hence, AB is an *area of distribution*; CD is an *area of re-distribution*; EF is an *area of accumulation* (as is also the overall action between 'C' and 'H'); and GH is an *area of re-accumulation*. Thus the two broad CMA categories, trend and congestion area, may be further sub-divided as follows:

1. Trend.
   a. Downtrend.
   b. Uptrend.

2. Congestion Area.
   a. Area of Distribution.
   b. Area of Re-distribution.
   c. Area of Accumulation.
   d. Area of Re-accumulation.

Within the overall action between 'C' and 'H', identified in the previous paragraph as an area of accumulation, is a briefer area of accumulation—EF. In actuality, rippling out from all protracted trends and congestion areas are briefer trends and congestion areas of progressively smaller scope, as in Illustration VIII.

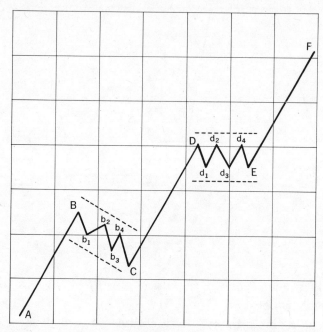

Illustration VIII

Illustration VIII portrays protracted uptrend AF and *some* of the subsidiary actions one would customarily expect to encounter within such an uptrend. AB, CD, and EF are briefer uptrends with b_1b_2, b_3b_4, d_1d_2, and d_3d_4 being *even* briefer uptrends. BC is a brief downtrend with Bb_1, b_2b_3, b_4C, Dd_1, d_2d_3, and d_4E being briefer downtrends. DE is a congestion area or, more definitively, an area of re-accumulation. BC might also be referred to as a major counter trend in the sense that it is a downtrend of substance running counter to the overall uptrend AF. Correspondingly, Bb_1, b_2b_3, b_4C, Dd_1, d_2d_3, and d_4E might also be referred to as minor counter trends. Even b_1b_2 and b_3b_4, despite running in the same direction as the overall trend, are counter trends to intermediate downtrend BC. Although these are all characteristic components of the CMA panorama, they by no means begin, in nature or complexity, to be all-representative or all-inclusive.

The following is a *Commodity Research Bureau* 'weekly' chart picturing the action of Soybean Oil for a little over 4 years:

As can be seen, Soybean Oil, in the summer of 1968, embarked upon a three-year bull market. This bull market, like most commodity bull markets, was far from being a one-way street. It suffered numerous interruptions of disparate severity. The interruptions, in turn, proliferated fluctuations of widely varying magnitude. Had the foregoing chart been a daily instead of a weekly one, the action portrayed would have been amplified by almost five times and, further, would have been correspondingly fragmented into fluctuations of even more widely varying magnitude.

In Chapter 4, traders were defined by the probable or anticipated time spans of their market commitments. Since no recognized standard exists for the definitive partitioning of time spans, the definitions applied were necessarily arbitrary. Time span definitions are also used to identify trends and, less frequently, congestion areas. Once again, by reason of the absence of any recognized standard, the definitions which follow are arbitrary:

MINI-TERM	Less than one week.
SHORT-TERM	One week to one month.
MEDIUM-TERM	One to three months.
LONG-TERM	Three months to one year.
MAXI-TERM	One year or longer.

A *scallop*'s eaten now and then.
A *wedge* is used by golfing men.
A *top* is oft a child's choice toy.
A *diamond* is a girl's best joy.
A *pennant*'s flown at college games.
A *flag* stirs patriotic flames.
If that is what you really think,
This chapter sure will make you blink.

8/Congestion Area Action

Positioning *uninterrupted* long-term and maxi-term trends is indisputably the easiest way to profitably trade commodity futures. Unfortunately, futures prices are congesting much more often (in a broad 3-month sense) than they are trending. Consequently, even would-be long-term trend followers are frequently prompted to seek those shorter trends that are usually contained by protracted (3-month plus) congestion areas. In addition, as rare as are long-term and maxi-term trends, long-term and maxi-term trends *without congestive interruptions of major importance* are virtually nonexistent. For these and other reasons which will become apparent as further material is presented, most CMA followers sooner or later become serious congestion area students.

To review, Congestion Areas fall into four categories:

1. Area of Distribution (or Top).
2. Area of Re-distribution (or Downtrend Consolidation Area).
3. Area of Accumulation (or Bottom).
4. Area of Re-accumulation (or Uptrend Consolidation Area).

A *congestion area* is sidewise price action within a trading range. It may either be a temporary interruption of a price trend (*consolidation area*), or it may be the final termination of a price trend (*top* or *bottom*). Congestion area action reflects the market's adjustment to a new price level that has evolved from prior trend action and results from the operation of supply and demand at this new level. A standoff between buyers and sellers may last but a short time, or for several years; but eventually either buying or selling will dominate to cause the price to emerge from the congestion area. A new trend will be thereby created.

Congestion areas have been submitted to considerably more exhaustive study than any other aspect of technical analysis. Two prime reasons have already been given. Another reason is that the proper identification of a clearly established congestion area enables a trader to know the direction of the trend destined some day to emerge. Also, a trader may initially be able to judge how long the congestion area is likely to last, and he may ultimately be able to judge how far the ensuing trend is likely to carry—pricewise or timewise. With such valuable information available from congestion area action, one would assume the problem of congestion area identification to be a complex one. Yet, where a congestion area is clearly established, its identity can only be one of two choices. Either:

1. A top or an area of re-accumulation, or
2. A bottom or an area of re-distribution.

Observe Illustration IX.

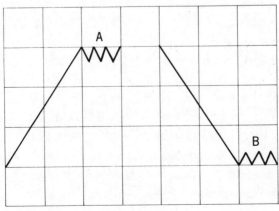

Illustration IX

In Illustration IX, congestion area A was proceeded by an up-trend. This congestion area, therefore, can obviously not qualify either as a bottom or as an area of re-distribution. Correspondingly, congestion area B can obviously not qualify either as a top or as an area of re-accumulation. Thus two problems, distinguishing tops from bottoms and distinguishing re-accumulation areas from re-distribution areas, never really existed in the first place.

Yet, the CMA of Illustration X can occur.

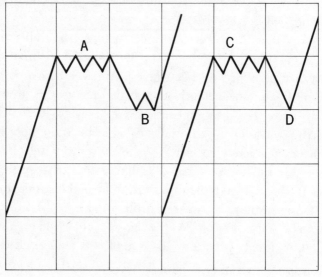

Illustration X

A price, like an army, sometimes advances (or retreats) too rap-idly for its own good. Then, unable to consolidate at the furthest point of an intermediate advance, a price is forced or prompted to retreat a short distance for additional consolidation (B). Sometimes, after a temporary retreat, a price is able to resume its major advance without any further consolidation (D). Although congestion areas A and C may be technically considered minor areas of distribution, they certainly cannot be regarded as tops or as areas of re-distribution. Indeed, it would seem more logical for AB and CD each to be taken as a whole and, as such, each to be considered as an area of re-accumulation. In technicians' jargon, these phenomena are known as *end runs*. An end run is a sudden trend reversal which soon fully pierces the congestion area from which the prior trend just recently emerged. An end run can occur at any point in CMA. End runs occurring subsequent to breakouts from congestion areas that contain no top or bottom characteristics are fairly easy to foresee, especially when they include additional consolidation as in (B). End runs occurring just above or below top or bottom formations, as in Illustration XI which follows, are far more difficult to anticipate and, correspondingly, pose much greater threats to traders:

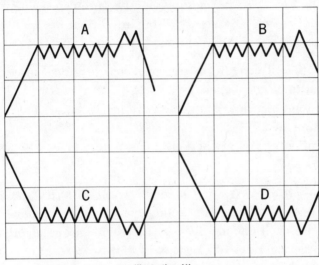

Illustration XI

When a price stalls shortly following a breakout and congests, as in A or C of Illustration XI, a trader is warned that the prior relationship between buyers and sellers may be in the process of a major alteration. Although, as already noted, such an end run constitutes a serious threat to traders, it commensurately presents a fine profit opportunity for those alert to the situation. When no such warning exists, as in B or D of Illustration XI, the threat is even greater and the profit opportunity much more difficult to recognize at an early stage. A and B are also known as *bull traps* and C and D as *bear traps*.

To solve either of the two problems that do exist, tops versus re-accumulation areas and bottoms versus re-distribution areas, technicians focus on trying to ascertain what formation or pattern an area in question resembles (or is beginning to resemble). If the developing pattern resembles a *head and shoulders*, then it is more likely to be a top than a re-accumulation area; or, if the developing pattern resembles a *descending triangle,* then it is more likely to be a re-distribution area than a bottom. Unfortunately, so few congestion areas can claim clear-cut resemblances to classic patterns that some at times are assigned a diversity of designations one might expect from a group taking the same Rorschach test. Fortunately, however, one does not have to rely exclusively upon pattern identification in order to solve the foregoing two problems. There are four other clues, though frequently disregarded, that are most useful in helping to solve the aforementioned two problems:

1. Location of congestion area in recent historical price range.
2. Breadth of congestion area.
3. Location of price change activity in the latter stage of a congestion area.
4. Location of volume action in the latter stage of a congestion area.

1. *Location of congestion area in recent historical price range.* In the previous chapter, an action consideration somewhat highlighted with each commodity was its recent historical price range. For example, the price of Cocoa, with but two exceptions, has been enclosed within a range of roughly 20¢ to 45¢ for over twenty years. This is not to say that inflation won't some day elevate that range, as it undoubtedly will; but until then, certain hypotheses may be drawn:

A. When Cocoa congests in the 20¢ area, the formation of a bottom may be reasonably anticipated.
B. When Cocoa congests near or beyond 40¢, the formation of a top may be reasonably anticipated.
C. When Cocoa congests between 25¢ and 35¢, a resultant consolidation area is more likely—but far from a certainty.

The same general hypotheses apply to the other commodity futures in varying degrees. However, because a few existing contracts have at one time been changed as to specifications of the subsumed products, some historical price ranges may be subject to slight distortions.

2. *Breadth of congestion area.* The breadth of a congestion area can be measured by price change activity (point and figure method)

as well as by time. In Illustration X, the congestion areas portrayed were areas of consolidation. In Illustration XI, the areas were tops and bottoms. The tops and bottoms were much broader than the consolidation areas. This was not an accident. Tops and bottoms almost always take longer to form than consolidation areas. In addition, although it was not so portrayed, bottoms usually take longer to form than tops. Timewise, consolidation areas rarely last more than a month; tops generally linger from one to six months; and bottoms may be in formation anywhere from one month to several years. It is true that the breadth of a congestion area cannot be measured until after a real breakout has occurred; but if the duration of a congestion area approaches patience-testing proportions, a trader should be prepared for the emergence of a *major* price trend reversal—the hallmark of tops and bottoms. Cocoa action in 1965 provides a unique exception. Following a major decline, Cocoa congested for over four years in the 20¢ to 25¢ area. This strongly indicated that the ensuing trend would be up. Instead, Cocoa plunged further down to 10¢. Copper has been a frequent exception since 1966 in that many of its bottoms and tops, timewise, have resembled consolidation areas.

3. *Location of price change activity in the latter stage of a congestion area.* In the initial stage of a congestion area after a substantial rise or decline, price fluctuations are apt to be wide and hectic in reflection of the market's struggle to adjust to a new price level. Later on, price fluctuations will assume more conventional characteristics. If price change activity then tends to occur toward the lower level of the congestion area, the implication is that important buying support is being given the market and that the next trend will thus be up. Conversely, if price change activity then tends to occur toward the upper level of the congestion area, the implication is that important selling pressure is being exerted on the market and that the next trend will thus be down.

4. *Location of volume action in the latter stage of a congestion area.* Although volume action and price change activity seldom supply clues concomitantly, there is a strong correlation in what their clues indicate and imply. Therefore, if heavier volume tends to occur toward the lower level of a congestion area in its latter stage of formation, the implication is that important buying support is being

given the market and that the next trend will thus be up; and if heavier volume tends to occur toward the upper level, the implication is that important selling pressure is being exerted on the market and that the next trend will thus be down. Volume action is so vital to CMA analysis that it will be examined in a separate chapter.

When congestion area patterns can be identified with some degree of unambiguity, they may be assigned varying amounts of weight in technical analysis. How much weight depends upon their clarity and conclusiveness in conjunction with all other relevant considerations. The patterns illustrated in the remainder of this chapter are the more conventional ones found in CMA. For general identification, they may be classified as either consolidation or price reversal (Illustration XII).

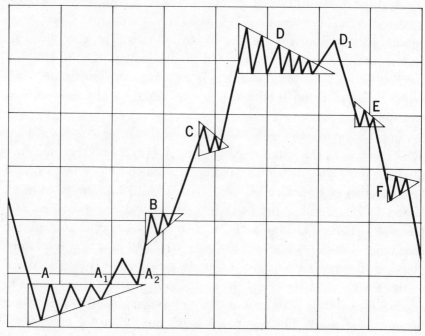

Illustration XII

Because, after a substantial rise or decline, price fluctuations initially are apt to be wide and hectic in reflection of the market's struggle to adjust to a new price level, and then will gradually simmer down, triangular formations occur with great frequency. In fact, the triangle is the only pattern that customarily turns up as both consolidation and price reversal. It is portrayed in Illustration XII enjoying its unique distinction of being able to appear at any point in CMA. In that illustration, A and D are major price reversals whereas B, C, E, and F are consolidations. More definitively, A is a bottom, D is a top, B and C are areas of re-accumulation, and E and F are areas of re-distribution.

A symmetrical or equilateral triangle, qua pattern, does not indicate the direction likely to be taken by the ultimately emerging trend. An ascending or descending triangle, however, does advertise its intention. An ascending triangle is normally bullish and a descending triangle normally bearish. Ascending triangles A and B are characteristically followed by uptrends with descending triangles D and E characteristically followed by downtrends.

The rationale of why ascending and descending triangles are endowed with bullish and bearish implications respectively is quite logical. The ascending triangle, for instance, conveys a simple picture of what happens when a growing demand for a certain commodity encounters a large offering at a particular price. If the demand persists, the offering will eventually be absorbed by new buyers, owners adding to their already held positions, and short coverers—all essentially anticipating higher price levels. After complete absorption of the subject offering, prices will advance rapidly. But before this happens, some owners will have been prompted to dispose of part or all their holdings, old shorts will have been tempted to increase their positions, and new shorts will have been lured into the market. These forces will have triggered a series of brief declines, which will then have attracted new demand, and which will in turn have stimulated a succession of rallies back up to the price where the large but gradually diminishing supply existed. Since the bullish forces predominated, each decline will have been met with new demand at progressively higher prices. Thus is formed what visually resembles an ascending triangle.

Triangle C is symmetrical and F is equilateral. They are thereby unendowed with pattern implications. Inasmuch as C is higher on the price scale than F, one might be prematurely inclined to play C for a bearish formation and F for a bullish one. Because consolidations far outnumber price reversals, the dominating clue here that should forestall such an error is the prior trend. In the case of C, the prior trend was up. This, by itself, favors the emergence of a trend in the same direction. The converse, of course, is true with F. A second weighty clue is the fact that neither C nor F had broadened sufficiently to suggest a major price reversal. Although it could not be known in advance that this would not occur, a broadening of scope should be allowed to evolve before taking seriously the possibility of a major price reversal.

A_1 and D_1, the upside breakouts from A and D, shortly assumed the characteristics of end runs. The decline after the A_1 breakout, however, halted and reversed itself at the apex of the triangular formation. This action canceled out the end run possibility. In addition, the ascendancy feature of the formation coupled with its low location on the price scale had already suggested that an end run was not likely to materialize. The decline after D_1, on the other hand, by-passed the apex of triangle D and promptly fell below it, thus rendering the end run a foregone conclusion. Correspondingly, the descendancy feature of the formation coupled with its high location on the price scale had already suggested that this particular action was indeed likely to materialize. Finally, the broadness of A and D strongly indicated that they would ultimately be a bottom and a top respectively.

Illustration XIII portrays classic consolidation patterns other than triangles.

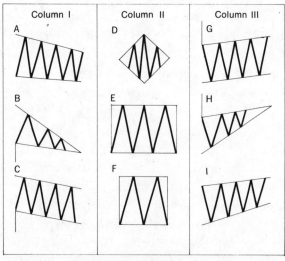

Illustration XIII

In Illustration XIII, the three patterns under Column I are bullish, the three under Column II neutral, and those under Column III bearish. A and I are *wedges*, B and H *pennants*, C and G *flags*; D is a *diamond*, E a *rectangle*, and F a *box*. Note that the pennants and flags, not unnaturally, are on the end of poles. This is supposed to mean that pennants and flags only occur after precipitous market moves. When a pennant or a flag occurs after a gentle and gradual market advance or decline, the orthodox technician will obediently try to visualize another pattern for identification purposes. Note also that a pennant is nothing more than a form of triangle. To qualify as a pennant, a triangle must not only be "masted," it must also have two of its sides slanting in the same direction; i.e., upward or downward. Of all the consolidation patterns, the ascending triangle is the most reliable to follow in an uptrend and, conversely, the descending triangle is the most reliable to follow in a downtrend. The wedge, however, is perhaps even more useful when spotted, for it is frequently the final consolidation area prior to the formation of a major price reversal.

It may seem contradictory that wedges, pennants, and flags customarily slope against the prevailing trend. It makes sense, though, when realized that a consolidation area is often simply an area of price corrective action caused by a market sprint which overran the price level that could then be supported by the law of supply and demand. Plainly speaking, corrective action is by implication trend countering.

Major price reversal patterns fall into four general categories:

1. Triangle.
2. Saucer.
3. V-Shape.
4. Platform.

The triangle has already been illustrated and discussed. The others follow.

Large saucers constitute gentle major price reversal action. Consequently, they occur far more frequently as bottoms than as tops. In Illustration XIV, A is a major bottom. B is a *platform* or a saucer *handle*. Sideways action immediately upon the breakout from a major saucer is a common patience-testing occurrence. Sometimes,

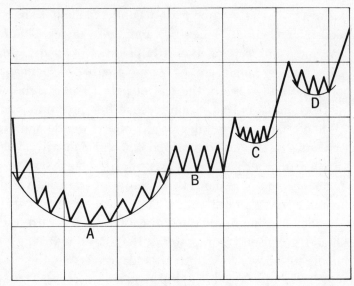

Illustration XIV

small saucer consolidations punctuate the trend emerging from a saucer price reversal. C and D are such saucers and are known as *scallops*. Of all the major price reversal patterns, the saucer is the most reliable to follow.

Although, as stated in the previous paragraph, major saucers "occur far more frequently as bottoms than as tops," the 1971 bull market in Orange Juice ended with an inverted saucer top, as shown below:

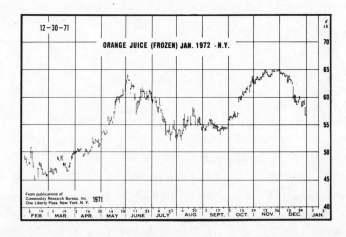

A few months later, some technicians were actually referring to the January-February action on the chart that follows as a saucer platform. The less astigmatic were simply calling it an ugly handle. One lesson to be learned from the January 7¢-rally is: Beware of being short Orange Juice during the Florida "freeze-threat" season, even in a major downtrend. A more important point underscored by this rally is the constant peril that confronts incautious pyramid builders.

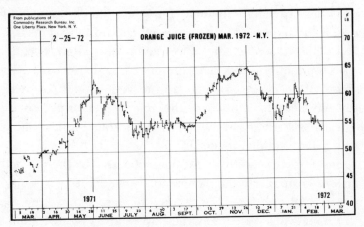

In Illustration XV, A is an *inverted V top*, B is an *M* or *double top*, and C is a *triple top*. Turn over the patterns and they would be, respectively, a V *bottom*, a W or *double bottom*, and a *triple bottom*.

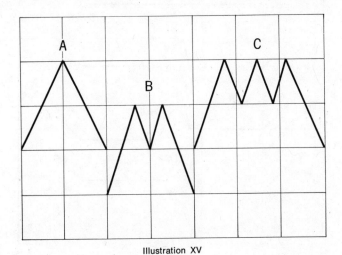

Illustration XV

Of all the major price reversals, the V pattern is by far the most hazardous to traders because it constitutes an irrevocable about-face with virtually no warning. In addition, a trend emerging from a V is the most difficult to board since the specter of a *double* pattern remains a distinct possibility until the new trend has been in existence long enough to justify an intermediate and perhaps important price correction. The V is characteristic of a market that has been emotionally fueled way beyond the bounds of rational values. Inasmuch as sellers are habitually more impatient than buyers, and while optimism is limited only by the sky whereas CMA pessimism is necessarily exhausted somewhere above zero, this pattern occurs more often as a top than as a bottom. The double and triple patterns also occur more often as tops, but not to the same extent. By reason of the intra-day activity implicit at the apices of such patterns, point and figure charts are generally more helpful than vertical line charts in spotting these sudden reversals.

Whereas tops are customarily characterized by hectic activity, bottoms are customarily characterized by moderating activity. For this reason, *platform* major price reversals are more often located at the terminals of downtrends than uptrends. In Illustration XVI,

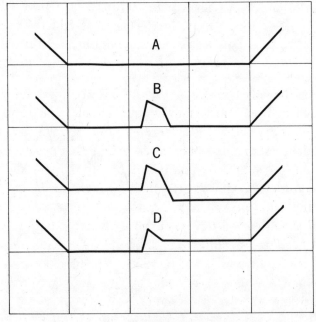

Illustration XVI

A is a *simple platform bottom*, B is a *compound platform bottom*, C is a *delayed ending platform bottom*, and D is a *duplex horizontal platform bottom*. Also, as illustrated, mid-platform rallies of substance are a feature of complex platform patterns.

The saucer-handle major price reversal, where the handle resembles a platform, might be said to be a *hybrid* pattern—a pattern that is merely a combination of a saucer and a simple platform. Illustration XVII pictures two other common hybrid patterns, A being a *delayed V ending bottom* and B being a *V extended bottom*. Each, obviously, is a combination of the simple platform and the V.

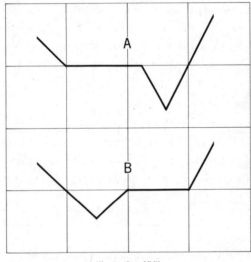

Illustration XVII

Note, in the chart on page 88, the classic V extended bottom formed by Hog prices in the late summer and early fall of 1971. Then note the classic inverted V top formed in early 1972. By observing the attendant volume and open interest figures, subjects which will be featured in Chapter 10, you will also note that the CMA at the top was considerably more hectic than the CMA at the bottom:

Of all the major price reversal patterns, the most renowned is the *head and shoulders*—a top when upright and a bottom when inverted. A head and shoulders can almost always be envisioned when the high point of a broad top or the low point of a broad bottom occurs somewhere near the middle of a formation. In other words, more heads and shoulders are products of imagination than reality. A much ballyhooed feature of the head and shoulders is, strangely,

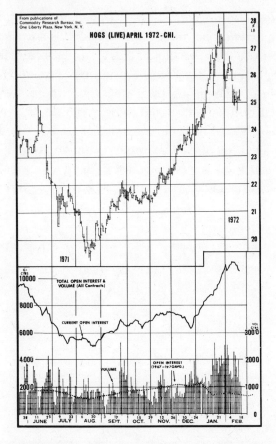

its *neckline*; strange because the neckline in a top, drawn tangent with the lows of the left and right shoulders, is located where it would more properly be termed an "upper chestline," or some such. It is the neckline that must be pierced by market action before the existence of a head and shoulders is validated. This pattern appears about equally as a bottom or top. To avoid further terminological confusion, however, the more common heads and shoulders one is apt to encounter are depicted in Illustration XVIII as tops. Also shown are the accessory necklines.

In Illustration XVIII, the H & S (head and shoulders) of A resemble platforms, of B saucers, and of C V-shapes. Rarely do all the components of a H & S conform to the same pattern or to clear-cut patterns. Usually, they are simply approximate semblances of two or three patterns with the final determination being the eyes of the beholder. D contains two left shoulders, E two right shoulders, and

F two heads. Observe that if F's left head were located slightly nearer the left shoulder, its identity would be in dispute. H & S patterns have been known to contain up to three (and even more) left or right shoulders or heads. Assuming three to be the ordinary maximum, there are twenty-seven possible H & S combinations wherein each of the basic components numbers from one to three. G has an ascending neckline and H a descending one. The upper extremity of G's right shoulder is on the same plane as the upper extremity of G's left shoulder, but it does not have to be. It could be either higher or lower, though unlikely to be lower in the face of an ascending neckline. The upper extremity of H's right shoulder is lower than the upper extremity of H's left shoulder, but, as with G, it need not be. An ascending neckline on a H & S is considered to be of little significance, but a descending neckline is thought to add bearishness to an already bearish picture. Conversely, an ascending neckline on an inverted H & S is thought to add bullishness to an already bullish picture. In I, point x locates the piercing of the neckline. This is widely regarded as an excellent selling opportunity. Sometimes there is a rally back to the plane on which the neckline exists, as indicated by point y. This is also widely regarded as an excellent

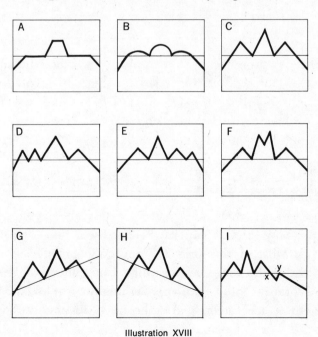

Illustration XVIII

selling opportunity when it occurs. Conversely, such points on an inverted H & S are widely regarded as excellent buying opportunities. A rally back to the neckline is least likely to occur when the neckline is of the descending variety; or, in the case of an inverted H & S, a decline back to the neckline is least likely to occur when the neckline is of the ascending variety.

In the latter months of 1971 and early months of 1972, Copper was widely thought to have formed an inverted H & S bottom. The head is easy to spot—the November action around 46¢. How about the shoulders? Two seem clear-cut with two others being possible candidates. And where should the neckline be drawn? Some premature visionaries were drawing it across the 50¢ level until the severe decline in late January canceled out that possibility. The two other possibilities at this point are a descending one and an ascending one as drawn:

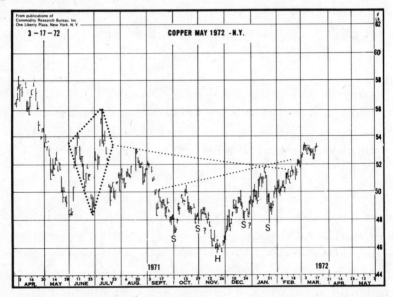

On the Copper chart, there was considerable congestion area action from May through August. Part of the action even resembles a diamond. Most of this prior-bottom-forming congestive activity occurred within the 50¢-54¢ price range. Consequently, after Copper turned up from 46¢ and began approaching the level where that congestive activity had taken place, the price advancing market was likely to run into periods of stormy weather. This it did, suffering a 2¢ decline in December, a 4¢ decline in January, and a bogging down in March. The reason such past action affects subsequent markets falls into four categories:

1. In the 50¢-54¢ price range, many premature Copper bulls had gotten hooked in the market. As the opportunity to get off the hook presented itself roughly half a year later, some of these longs were eager to get out whole from what had been a sticky trading experience.

2. There were also some Copper bears who had partly or altogether missed the boat on the short side when Copper was selling above 50¢. Those still bearish were now being given a second opportunity at the very same pier from which the boat had previously sailed.

3. Also missing the boat, partly or altogether, were some dealers in the physical product who had failed to satisfactorily hedge their inventories. Those too, whose minds had not changed, were now being afforded a second opportunity.

4. Finally, of course, the advance from 46¢ to the 50¢-54¢ price range was destined to attract some brand new shorts and hedgers as well as some previous shorts and hedgers who had in the meantime covered at a profit, and, in addition, was destined to induce some profit-taking by longs who had bought Copper at prices below 50¢.

In a declining market, similar congestion area action would tend to thwart the decline for the converse of these four causative categories. Incidentally, dealers who employ the futures market for hedging purposes not only go short to hedge an inventory they fear may become too heavy at then prevailing prices, but also go long to hedge an inventory they fear may become too light at then prevailing prices.

Past congestive activity that may stall or reverse an advancing price is known as an *area of resistance*. Conversely, such activity that may stem or reverse a declining price is known as an *area of support*. The location of significant past congestion areas, even those going back over ten years, is viewed with considerable importance by technicians. Broad congestion areas that evolve as major bottoms can become permanent price barriers. Broad congestion areas that evolve as major tops can become price barriers for a generation or more. The best source for locating significant distant past congestion areas is the long-term *continuation* charts published by the *Commodity Research Bureau*. Since the life of most futures contracts is no more than eighteen months, minor bottoms, minor tops, and most consolidation areas will have but nominal influence on the market beyond that length of time. However, as already demonstrated, even relatively insignificant consolidation areas, when young, can impressively affect the course of the market for perhaps up to a year.

The 1971-1972 Orange Juice saga continues to provide illustrative points. On the chart that follows, observe the area of re-accumulation (or uptrend consolidation area) that spanned from mid July to mid October 1971. It was precisely this congestive activity, to the technician, that thrust back the downtrend in January 1972 to the extent of 7¢. And after returning to the level of that prior congestive activity six weeks later, it took still another month before the subject consolidation area could be finally penetrated:

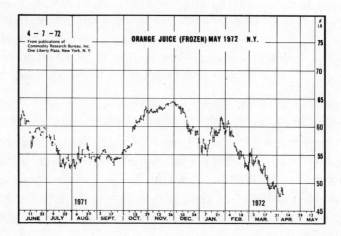

Technicians have long wrestled with the question: How far will a price, emerging from a congestion area, advance or decline? The only method that has consistently enjoyed a useful degree of success is the point and figure. Called the *count*, this term means counting the squares across a P & F plotted congestion area to ascertain the likely approximate extent of the subsequent advance or decline. The premise here is that there is a definite correlation between the width of a P & F plotted congestion area and the vertical extent of the ensuing price movement that emerges from it. Once again drawing upon the Orange Juice saga, Illustration XIX is a 1¢ P & F picture of the priorly discussed 1971 mid July-mid October re-accumulation area.

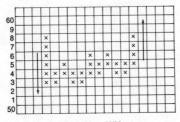

Illustration XIX

Although the mid July-mid October action for 1971 Orange Juice may permanently be labeled an area of re-accumulation, it is only a support area so long as the price of Orange Juice remains at 53¢ or above. Once the price falls below 53¢, which it substantially did in March of 1972, the subject area becomes one of resistance. This means that, after the decline below 53¢, any Orange Juice price rise approaching 53¢ within the next eighteen months or so will have to contend with that 53¢-56¢ congestive activity.

The congestion area in Illustration XIX is well-defined. It ranges from 53¢ to 56¢ and is bounded by two unmistakable walls whose lower portions are part of and vertically circumscribe the pattern. This congestion area became established as an uptrend consolidation area or re-accumulation area upon the upward surge from the 56¢ level. Do not expect all congestion areas to be as easy to delineate.

The crucial issue in determining the count is the selection of the price level within the subject congestion area. It is seldom that one particular level is clearly indicated. The two most common qualifications are:

1. The price level that contains the most "x"ed squares.
2. A price level that reaches both walls, where two walls exist.

The 54¢ level contains the most "x"ed squares, nine, but falls a square short of reaching the right wall. The 55¢ and 56¢ levels extend to both walls but contain fewer "x"ed squares than the 54¢ level, eight and four respectively. The 53¢ level contains only four "x"ed squares and extends less than half way to the right wall. It would thus seem that the 54¢ and 55¢ levels qualify as the leading count candidates.

The count across the 54¢ level is ten and thereby suggests an ultimate price advance to 64¢. The eleven count across the 55¢ level indicates a rise to 66¢. Orange Juice actually topped out at 64¢. This validated the count at the 54¢ level. Even the count at the 55¢ level was only off by 2¢. Such pinpoint accuracy is a rarity, but target areas located by the count method that are within the realm of reality are valid with a consistency that compels them to be taken seriously.

Before the upward move from 56¢, it was far from an absolute certainty that the subject congestion area would turn out to be one of re-accumulation. Its P & F configuration in conjunction with the count, however, did weigh in favor of an ultimate advance. Observe the activity at the upper level of the pattern—56¢. The plots are scattered and therefore generally regarded as being relatively meaningless. Now observe the activity at the lower level of the pattern —53¢. The four plots here are compactly located within a lateral range of five squares. Compact activity at the lower level of a congestion area wherein the activity at the upper level has been scattered implies, to many P & F technicians, a forthcoming upside breakout. In addition, if the count across that lower level can sustain a move to a level somewhere above the pattern, an upside breakout becomes an even greater likelihood. In this case, the count is five. If fulfilled, the promised advance would reach 58¢, 2¢ above the pattern's upper level.,

A ½ ¢ or other type of P & F chart might have afforded a slightly clearer or different picture as might also a chart of another contract month. Some technicians have been known to spend many of their evenings and weekends constructing and analyzing virtually every reasonably imaginable chart of those commodities in which they are interested. The only objective comment that can be made about such an investment of energy must be dictated by the bottom-line results of each thus inclined technician.

If a consolidation area count is valuable, a major reversal area count is indeed invaluable. The principal reason, of course, is the far greater profit opportunity afforded by the trend that emerges from a major reversal area. Observe Illustration XX, a 2¢ P & F chart of the July 1971 Corn top that spans from August 1970 to March 1971.

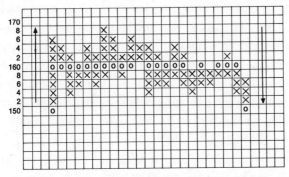

Illustration XX

The foregoing pattern has the characteristics of a platform top. It is bounded on the left by a wall and on the right by two partitions. The $1.56, $1.58, $1.60, and $1.62 levels are the only logical count candidates, but the greater activity at the $1.58 and $1.60 levels elects them. There are twenty-two squares across both these levels; however, because the chart is a 2¢ one, the lateral count must be doubled. The subtraction of the doubled lateral count (forty-four) from $1.58 and from $1.60 results in a count down to $1.14 and $1.16 respectively. Seven months later, Corn touched $1.20. Interestingly, the count from the less qualified $1.62 level is precisely $1.20.

Many regard the count as an inexplicable phenomenon. Other than the fact that there is no such thing as an inexplicable phenomenon in any market place, in support of the count is a wealth of logic. Part of this logic stems from technical factors and part from fundamental factors.

As to some of the principal technical factors, first consider an uptrend consolidation area. The price of a commodity is on the rise but is currently stalled—congesting in preparation for a continuance of that rise. On the correct side of the market, some old longs are being replaced by new longs for a variety of reasons. Essentially, the new longs enjoy more confidence in a further market rise than the longs they are replacing. Is it not logical to presume that the more such replacement activity goes on, the higher will be that further market rise? The converse, of course, is true with a downtrend consolidation area.

Next consider a bottom. The price of a commodity has suffered an extended decline and is currently congesting in preparation for a major reversal. This time the old longs were premature in taking their positions and are now saddled with paper losses. Most of those who persevere will be eagerly liquidating their positions as their get-even points are approached or reached. For this reason, these longs will be exerting a sobering influence on any subsequent market rise. During the formation of the bottom, however, impatience, disenchantment, disgust, and other factors will gradually prompt many of these longs to give up on the market and accordingly jettison their positions. Their replacements will be longs who not only enjoy greater confidence in the market, but who are also unbridled by disheartening paper losses. As with the considerations in the foregoing paragraph, is it not logical to presume that the more such replacement activity goes on, the higher will be the ultimate market rise? And the converse, of course, is true with a top.

The fundamental economic factors that support the logic of the count play their most important roles at the tops and bottoms of market place price swings. A top constitutes a price level which will ultimately prove to have been unduly inflated. A bottom constitutes a price level which will ultimately prove to have been unduly deflated. Unduly inflated and unduly deflated prices exert a crucially powerful impact on producers and consumers alike. The longer such prices persist, the greater the resultant impact.

Any commodity can be used for illustration. The details would be different, but the principles would be the same. An unduly inflated price for a commodity will quickly induce producers of that commodity to expand their production of it in every conceivable way. If the commodity is Copper, productive mines will begin to be worked around the clock, marginal mines will become more attentively managed, and previously unproductive mines will now be rehabilitated. In addition, the Copper mining business will lure back some former Copper miners as well as attract some neophytes. If the commodity is Wheat, many farmers will be induced to divert to Wheat uncultivated acreage or acreage priorly intended for other crops, and many marginal and unproductive Wheat farmers about to leave the business will now be persuaded to stay in it a while longer. Also, there will be former Wheat farmers again tempted to try their hands at growing this suddenly precious grain as well as visionary newcomers rushing to buy land in the Wheat Belt. With "bush" crops, inaccessibility, condition, and other considerations normally cause portions to remain unpicked (or ungathered). At unduly inflated prices, nothing remains unpicked. On the demand side, consumers will be induced to postpone purchases, to make do, to use less, to find substitutes, and so forth. Therefore, the longer an unduly inflated commodity price persists, the greater the entrance into the economy of facilities to produce that commodity and the greater the exit from the economy of consumer preference for that commodity. Translated into CMA, the longer an unduly inflated commodity price persists, the further will be its ultimate decline.

Conversely, an unduly deflated price for a commodity will step by step eliminate all but that commodity's most productive facilities, and even *their* operations will be curtailed. On the demand side, consumer preference will gradually be rebuilt until the reduced productive facilities can no longer satisfy it. Translated into CMA, the longer an unduly deflated commodity price persists, the further will be its ultimate rise. Thus is the count supported by fundamental economic factors as well as by technical ones.

Occasionally a commodity price becomes immensely inflated or immensely deflated. An immensely inflated price incites such a frantic expansion of production facilities that it usually peaks and then turns down as precipitously as it had risen. An immensely deflated price, on the other hand, incites such a frantic contraction of production facilities that it *sometimes* peaks (invertedly) and then turns up as precipitously as it had declined. Deflated prices usually stay down longer than inflated prices stay up because it usually takes longer to absorb an "oversupply" than it takes to sate an "overdemand." On a chart, an abrupt turnabout would appear either as an inverted V top or as a V bottom. Neither lends itself to the count. However, when an inverted V top or a V bottom occurs at an immensely inflated or immensely deflated price level, the ensuing price move may logically be expected to be far greater than it would have been had the price halted at a less extreme level. In other words, the more inflated a price becomes, the further will be its ultimate decline; and the more deflated a price becomes, the further will be its ultimate rise. Illustration XXI is a broad general portrayal of typical CMA that results from unduly and immensely deflated and inflated prices.

In Illustration XXI, AB and EF represent unduly deflated price periods whereas CD represents an unduly inflated price period. Note throughout that prices tend to stay down longer than they tend to stay up. Failure of the price to hold at EF results in a delayed ending, the entire bottom formation spanning from E to H with H approximating the uppermost level of congestion area EF. The price collapse to G, with its attendant further contraction of production facilities, is perhaps the principal cause of the subsequent rise to immensely inflated price I. Immensely inflated price I, in turn, with its attendant frantic expansion of production facilities, is perhaps the principal cause of the price collapse to J and the persistence of that immensely deflated price for the period from J to K. This immensely deflated price coupled with its persistence ultimately vaults the price back to immensely inflated price L.

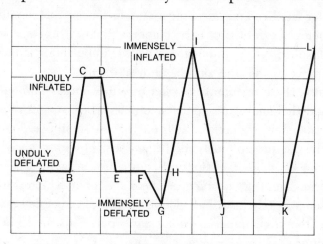

Illustration XXI

Observe from the long-term Sugar chart which follows that the preceding illustration somewhat accurately reflects Sugar's general price history for the nineteen plus years beginning with 1953:

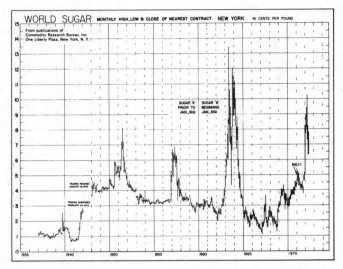

Various types of stop orders were discussed in Chapter 6. A stop order is used for three purposes:

1. To limit losses.
2. To protect paper profits.
3. To enter the market.

No matter what the purpose, most stop orders are placed just above or just below a congestion area. The logic behind this is self-evident. The breakout from a congestion area is widely thought to herald a further move in the direction of that breakout.

Actually, these breakout points are so universally known to those concerned that they frequently turn out to be traps. This is not to suggest that stops should not be used at these seemingly logical locations. The user of stops at such locations, however, should be on notice that he will have plenty of company with which to exchange sympathy whenever thus trapped. One should also be on notice that the presence of this company will often result in mangled executions. Happily, though, a breakout point is necessary to the birth of most trend action.

Before proceeding to trend action analysis, it should be emphasized that congestion areas are not merely breath-catching berths for trends, at least not to many traders. Whereas a trend is an opportunity to realize one enormous profit essentially by sitting tight, a congestion area is an opportunity to realize many small profits by alert activity over the congestion area's life. In a well-defined congestion area, each decline to its lower limit constitutes a buy point and each rise to its upper limit constitutes a sell point. In a congestion area that lasts over six months, and some last for years, dozens of fairly clear-cut buying and selling opportunities present themselves. A ten-cent move in Pork Bellies is a substantial move, but the swings in a six-month Pork Belly congestion area may amount to well over a dollar.

Was I not bright
To buy and buy
When told this vivid tale?
Supply is tight
Demand is high,
The uptrend will prevail.
But then it slid
And hit the dust
With a most sick'ning thud.
Where is that kid
Who said I must
Plunge with my very blood?

9/Trend Action

Some trends are straight, some are curved; some are irregular or
poorly defined, and others are quite orderly and amazingly uniform.
A trend's principal characteristic is successive highs and lows attain-
ing levels above (in the case of uptrends) and below (in the case
of downtrends) their previous highs and lows. When three or more
lows during an uptrend (or, conversely, three or more highs during
a downtrend) can be roughly connected by a straight line, a trend
line is said to exist.

The uptrend action in figure A of Illustration XXII is ideal. Each
setback reverses itself precisely at the trend line and each high
reaches above its previous high. The downtrend action in figure C
is also ideal. Such ideal trend action is rare. More typically, trend
action will simulate the irregular spurts and setbacks pictured in
figure B. Beneath irregular action of this kind an objective trend
line cannot be drawn. As this one was drawn, two of the lows were
actually bisected by it. When trend action is so irregular that even

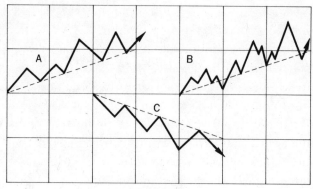

Illustration XXII

an approximate trend line cannot be satisfactorily drawn, then an internal trend line may be useful (Illustration XXIII).

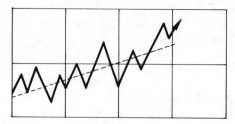

Illustration XXIII

Where a trend line exists and a parallel line can be drawn to roughly connect three or more highs (in the case of an uptrend) or three or more lows (in the case of a downtrend), a *trend channel* is said to exist. The example in Illustration XXIV of an uptrend channel is, of course, an oversimplification of CMA:

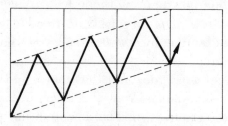

Illustration XXIV

A well-defined trend channel, like a well-defined congestion area, affords excellent trading opportunities. Each time the lower wall is touched or closely approached would be a buy point and each time the upper wall is touched or closely approached would be a sell point. Ironically, a serious penetration of either wall denotes a danger signal to the overall prevailing trend. In an uptrend channel, a serious penetration of the lower wall has an obvious bearish implication; but a serious penetration of the upper wall also has a bearish implication, although not as obvious a one. A penetration of the upper wall in an uptrend channel (or of the lower wall in a downtrend channel), if sustained, constitutes a *trend acceleration*. A trend acceleration, which can also occur without the existence of a prior channel, often signals the final stage of a bull or bear market. In Illustration XXV, A is a trend acceleration that has emerged from a trend channel whereas B is a trend acceleration that is simply an extension of the prevailing trend.

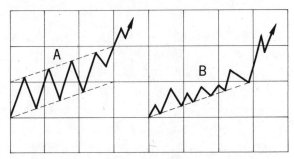

Illustration XXV

As indicated in Chapter 7, there are trends within trends. Contained in a maxi-term trend may be one or more long-term trends, which in turn may contain one or more medium-term trends, which in turn may contain one or more short-term trends, and which in turn may contain one or more mini-term trends. Trends are constantly being broken, either by counter trends or by congestion areas. The shorter the trend, the less significant its termination to the overall price structure. Illustration XXVI, on page 104, shows the trends-within-trends panorama.

AA_1 is a maxi-term uptrend that subsumes all the action depicted in Illustration XXVI. AB, and B_1 to the point that intersects A_1D_9, are long-term uptrends. B_1 to the point that intersects D_3D_4 is a medium-term uptrend. B_1 to slightly beyond C_7, and DD_1, are short-term uptrends. In fact, the action from B_1 to slightly beyond C_7 is

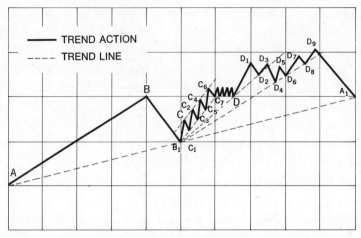

Illustration XXVI

walled by an uptrend channel. B_1C, C_1C_2, C_3C_4, C_5C_6, D_2D_3, D_4D_5, D_6D_7, and D_8D_9 are mini-term uptrends. Whichever very small uptrends in congestion area C_6D that subsume less than one day's action might be designated micro-term uptrends. BB_1 and D_9A_1 are short-term counter trends or short-term downtrends. The rest of the counter trends are of the mini or micro variety.

One may logically expect a strong correlation between the length of time a trend prevails and the extent to which its subsumed price advances or declines. To complicate matters, this correlation does not always exist—especially in CMA. For instance, from the beginning of December 1971 to the beginning of March 1972, in just three months, Sugar rose from a fraction over 5¢ to a fraction over 10¢. The related trend line barely qualified as long-term. Just as there have been spectacular commodity price moves within brief periods of time, there have also been modest price moves over long-term or maxi-term lengths of time. Consequently, a second set of designations is required to identify trends by the extent of their price moves as contradistinct from their duration:

1. Major Trend—50% or over for price advances and 33% or over for price declines.
2. Intermediate Trend—from 10% to 50% for price advances and from 10% to 33% for price declines.
3. Minor Trend—from 3% to 10% for either price advances or price declines.

4. Nominal Trend—Less than 3% for either price advances or price declines.

The reason for the different major and intermediate price advance and price decline percentage figures is that a move from 12 to 18 constitutes a 50% advance whereas the equal retracement from 18 to 12 constitutes but a 33% decline. No adjustment seems necessary for minor and nominal price advances or declines. The point to remember is the possibility of being confronted with trends of such combinative characteristics as major medium-term and minor maxi-term.

Nominal price moves or trends are occurring all the time and can thus be found anywhere in the CMA panorama. Essentially, nominal trends constitute the CMA of which congestion areas are made. Minor trends are sometimes found in congestion areas but more often connect them. Intermediate trends are almost always found connecting bottoms or tops with consolidation areas, or directly connecting bottoms with tops. Major trends are nearly always found connecting bottoms with tops. A major trend usually emerges from a bottom wherein the price has been unduly depressed for an extended period of time or a top wherein the price has simply been unduly elevated. As indicated in the previous chapter, the time element is considerably less important with tops than with bottoms as it generally takes so much less time to form tops than to form bottoms. The steeper a trend's angle of ascent or descent, the sooner that trend will reach its ultimate price objective and, correspondingly, the shorter will be that trend's life.

The crucial issue with which a trader must constantly wrestle is the pinpointing of buy and sell points that will enable him to board trends with maximum opportunities for profits at minimum risks. To do so, each trader develops his own style. There are, however, eight popular categorical methods of profiting from trend action.

1. *Bucking a trend in anticipation of its reversal.*

A trader will frequently buck a counter trend to enable him to board the overall larger trend (figure A of Illustration XXVII). Trend-bucking, however, is mostly employed to profit from nominal price swings within congestion areas and trend channels (figures B and C of Illustration XXVII). As a price approaches the upper or

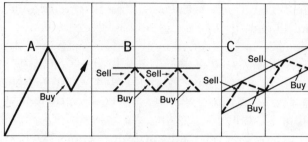

Illustration XXVII

lower limit of a congestion area or one of a trend channel's walls, a trader may buck the then prevailing nominal trend on the premise that the price will continue to remain within its prior confines. By virtue of the customary narrowness of congestion areas and trend channels, lucrative trading therein requires a great deal of trend-bucking.

Bucking any trend implies the anticipation of its termination in V or inverted V fashion. Such sudden reversals rarely occur with major trends, sometimes occur with intermediate trends, more often occur with minor trends, and frequently occur with nominal trends. Also, sudden reversals terminate counter trends slightly more often than they terminate trends heading in the same direction as the overall trend. To sum up, a V or inverted V formation will terminate in order of frequency: nominal counter trend, nominal trend, minor counter trend, minor trend, intermediate counter trend, intermediate trend, and major trend.

2. *Boarding a trend during a period of its consolidation in anticipation of the trend's subsequent continuance.*

Illustration XXVIII

The biggest danger here is that the anticipated consolidation area does not turn out to be one at all, but evolves instead as a top or bottom. A long-term consolidation area is a rarity in CMA. Therefore, sideways action that extends beyond three months should be regarded with suspicion. Most consolidation area trend-boarding is done by those who already enjoy sizable profits in the market. New position-takers tend to be scarce since they are apt to view the market as one in which they have already "missed the boat."

3. *Buying during the formation of a bottom or selling during the formation of a top.*

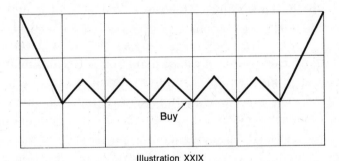

Illustration XXIX

The biggest danger here, of course, is that the anticipated bottom or top evolves instead as a consolidation area. Even barring such an unpleasant event, buying in a bottom area can tie up one's money for a considerable length of time. Positioning in a top area is also apt to tie up one's money, but not for as long a time. There are two principal advantages to positioning in bottom and top areas. First, one's risk is easier to calculate and limit. Taking a position after a trend emerges runs the greater risk of a nasty loss owing to a breakout failure or a sizable, though temporary, paper loss from a counter trend. Second, many traders believe it advantageous to take modest positions in bottom and top areas even at the risk of having their funds tied up for a while longer than they'd like. In so doing, as the reasoning goes, a trader will have "his feet wet" by the time the trend finally emerges—meaning that the paper profit from his initial position will instill in him the courage to more aggressively increase that position.

4. Buying or selling at congestion area breakout points.

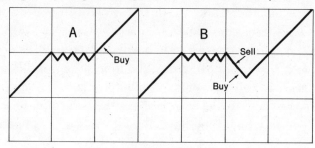

Illustration XXX

Positioning at a consolidation area breakout point (as in figure A of Illustration XXX), instead of during the period of consolidation, sacrifices the initial portion of the ensuing move but may be safer because an overall trend is sometimes punctuated by a consolidation area followed by a brief counter trend (as in figure B of Illustration XXX). When a counter trend does materialize, positioning it at its inception constitutes a bucking of the overall trend and promises at best a small profit. Bucking the counter trend should be more lucrative.

Before a trend finally emerges from a bottom or a top, it probably will have had a few false starts. Each of these false starts will have seemed at the time to be a breakout point to some traders. Those prompted to take positions will in turn find themselves sitting with a paper loss as well as a loss of the use of some of their money. Being able to distinguish between a false breakout and a valid one requires judgment fueled by a great deal of knowledge and experience.

Any 3% breakout from the upper price of a bottom or lower price of a top ($1.50 on a $50 price) should be regarded as potentially important. In Illustration XXXI, the upside breakout from bottom A, as indicated by the word *buy*, and the upside breakout from bottom B, as indicated by the word *buy* followed by a question mark, may both be considered to exceed 3%. Although these bottoms are virtually identical, the breakout from A is much more promising than the breakout from B—for two reasons:

In the first place, a series of congestion areas just prior to the formation of bottom B hovers menacingly over any upside trend action emerging from that formation. Quite likely, a few false starts fol-

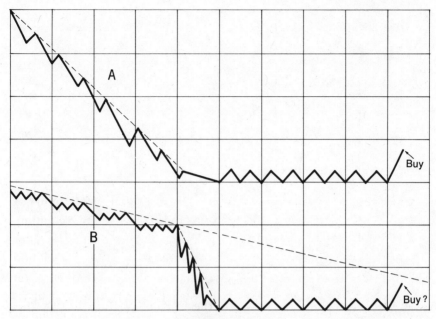

Illustration XXXI

lowed by a further broadening of the bottom will be required before
the overhead resistance can be fully penetrated. No such congestion
areas threaten upside trend action emerging from bottom A. In the
second place, the overall downtrend that preceded the formation of
bottom B is still in existence, whereas the overall downtrend that
preceded the formation of bottom A was broken at the outset of
bottom A's establishment. Such considerations as these crucially
influence the judgment of a trader.

All downtrends that precede the formation of a bottom are, of
course, ultimately broken. A brief downtrend was broken at the
outset of bottom B's establishment in Illustration XXXI. An overall
downtrend is sometimes broken at the outset of a bottom's establishment, as in A of Illustration XXXI, at times it is broken somewhere in the middle of a bottom formation, and at times near the
end of it. When the breaking of a prior overall downtrend coincides
with an upside breakout, as indicated by the word *buy* followed by
an exclamation mark in Illustration XXXII, that breakout point is
generally viewed with enthusiasm. Conversely, all the aforementioned bottom considerations apply about as equally to tops.

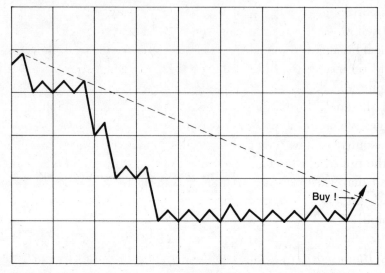

Illustration XXXII

In Illustration XXXII, note the two false starts prior to the valid breakout. There is also some congestion area action hovering above this bottom. It should not be much of a deterrent, however, to the forthcoming upside trend action.

5. *Buying or selling upon the breaking of the first minor counter trend after a breakout from a bottom or a top.*

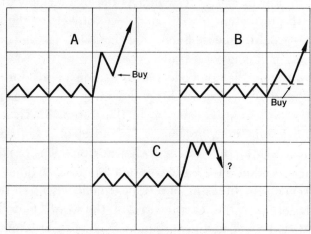

Illustration XXXIII

In order not to get trapped by a false breakout, to increase a prior holding, or for other reasons, a trader may use a trend's first setback as a positioning point. For many, also, it's easier to buy on weakness and sell on strength than vice versa. In Illustration XXXIII, A is a typical breakout followed by a brief counter trend. In B, the counter trend returns to the outer limit of the prior congestion area before forging ahead. This is a frequent occurrence, especially with head and shoulders formations. When there is a breakout followed by congestive action and then a counter trend, as in C, be wary. The breakout may have been a trap. Other than the trap possibility of C, the principal drawback of this trend-boarding method is that the trend may speed ahead without encountering a setback of signifi-cance until a substantial portion of the price move has been left behind.

6. *Buying or selling immediately upon perceiving an uptrend or downtrend.*

This Sugar chart portrays only a partial picture of the bottom action that preceded the December 1971 breakout. The actual bot-tom took seven years to form. Only a continuation chart could show that much action. Although the breakout seems to have occurred sometime between September and December, its validity was not established until the breakaway action on December 10. Sugar then sped skyward so rapidly that the only way to get aboard was simply to jump quickly aboard. There were neither consolidation areas nor counter trends to accommodate the slow of foot. Unfortunately, the memory of this breakaway will prompt many traders over the next few years to jump aboard other trends prematurely or at otherwise untimely moments.

7. *Gap action positioning procedure.*

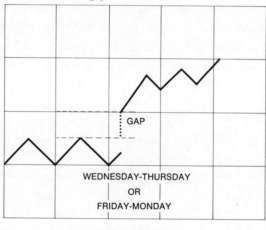

Illustration XXXIV

Gap action can occur at any point in the CMA panorama. A *gap*, which is generally considered as being created "overnight," is nothing more than an opening jump or drop in price that is higher or lower than the previous day's or session's high or low price. A gap resulting from a jump in price is an *upside gap* whereas a gap resulting from a drop in price is a *downside gap*. When one or more transactions subsequently take place that fully retrace the price jump or drop, the gap is then said to be *filled*. Most gaps are filled within short periods of time. The action that results from those gaps that are destined to remain unfilled for extended lengths of time is predictable with a phenomenal consistency.

There are four types of gaps:

1. Common.
2. Breakaway.
3. Runaway or Measuring.
4. Exhaustion.

In Illustration XXXV, A, B, G, and H are common gaps; C is a break-

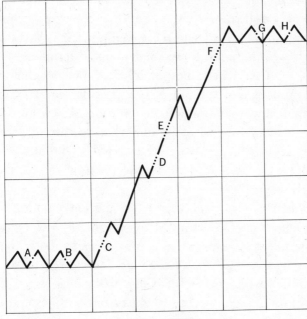

Illustration XXXV

away gap; D and E are runaway or measuring gaps; and F is an exhaustion gap.

Common gaps occur within well-defined congestion areas. The sole value of a common gap is to the trader who seeks to gain on the premise that the gap will be shortly filled. Subsequent to an upside common gap, such a trader might take a short position in anticipation of nothing more than a small but hopefully quick profit. The converse would be true of a downside common gap. A trap gap, as in Illustration XXXVI, is nothing more than a breakaway gap that fails to produce a trend. The gap, instead, becomes part of the overall

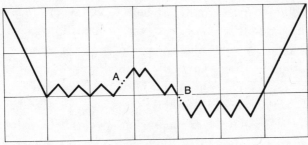

Illustration XXXVI

congestion area which for a moment it seemed to have terminated. It is thus converted from a breakaway gap back to a common one.

In Illustration XXXVI, A and B are common gaps. At the time they occurred, however, the gaps seemed to have terminated the congestive activity from which they emerged. In fact, the failure of trap gap A to produce an uptrend was a possible contributory cause to trap gap B and the resultant penetration of the lows that had hitherto prevailed. Instead of producing a downtrend, trap gap B simply inaugurated further congestive activity—but at a lower level. The overall bottom formation that evolved was of the classic delayed ending type.

Most breakaway gaps occur at the termination of bottoms and tops with occasional ones occurring at the termination of consolidation areas. Downside breakaway gaps occur more frequently than upside breakaway gaps. Also, they are generally larger. The larger the gap, the greater the confidence with which the incipient trend may be followed. In fact, large breakaway gaps from bottoms and tops may be followed with greater confidence than virtually any other category of CMA. The problem is that a large breakaway gap will have already seemingly consumed a material portion of the price move. This in itself acts as a psychological deterrent to many traders. If a 20¢ item is suddenly priced at 22¢ with no intervening sales, it is understandably difficult to jump in and buy. But that particular purchase is probably the surest bet available in CMA.

Most runaway or measuring gaps occur approximately midway in substantial price moves. When properly identified, a trader can pretty accurately estimate the remaining extent of the move then in progress. Although found almost exclusively within major or intermediate trend action, these gaps are not a consistent characteristic of such action. Consequently, when runaway or measuring gaps appear, they are often suspect of being exhaustion gaps.

Exhaustion gaps occur near the end of major or intermediate trend action. Although they cannot be immediately identified with full conviction, any conversion of the prior overall trend into extended congestive action should promptly dispel the possibility that these gaps are of the runaway or measuring species. The exhaustion gap is an unmistakable signal that the time to depart the prevailing trend is close at hand, but it is not necessarily a signal that one's position should be reversed. If the exhaustion gap occurs at the termination of a major or intermediate downtrend, it may be months or years before an uptrend emerges from the ensuing bottom formation. If the exhaustion gap occurs at the termination of a major or intermediate uptrend, the time element may be much shorter—but it still can be patience testing. In addition, a certain amount of upside action can yet be in the offing after an upside exhaustion gap with the converse being equally true after a downside exhaustion gap.

An *island reversal* formation is simply price activity that is isolated by an exhaustion gap on one side and a breakaway gap on the other. A one-day island reversal is a rarity, but has occurred. Most island reversals take from a few days to several months to form. Island reversals occur infrequently. When they do occur, however, the ensuing action is beautifully predictable.

In Illustration XXXVII, A is a textbook example of an island reversal—the exhaustion gap and the breakaway gap being right below the top and on the same plane without any intervening action filling the exhaustion gap. In B, the uptrend continued a bit before stalling into a top. The two gaps, therefore, are on a different plane. In C, the breakaway gap occurred within the top formation. It thus appeared at first to be a common gap. In D, there was intervening price activity that filled the exhaustion gap.

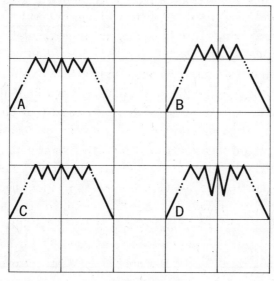

Illustration XXXVII

The 1968 Pork Belly market, as compared with other years, was a rather dull affair for many months. During these months there were a number of common gaps, all soon filled. A breakaway gap in late March gave birth to an intermediate medium-term uptrend. Within seven weeks, an inverted V top island reversal was formed. By July, the price erosion had exceeded 33% which thereby qualified the short-lived downtrend as a major one.

The Plywood market was a dull affair from its inception until early 1971. Then breakaway gaps that triggered a dramatic inter-

mediate medium-term uptrend multiplied its following virtually overnight. The prompt round-trip of Plywood prices characterized this commodity as a trading vehicle well worth watching by players with strong stomachs.

In October 1967, Orange Juice took off with four limit moves up. The hurricane season was about over and the freeze season was a couple of months away, but a serious drought had suddenly gripped Florida. To board the uptrend with 8¢ of the move already consumed seemed difficult to many. The enormous breakaway gap (or gaps), however, still had more than a 15¢ price advance to generate. Although the uptrend was of major proportions, it was of but medium-term duration. Note the small downside breakaway gap that inaugurated the trend's quick reversal.

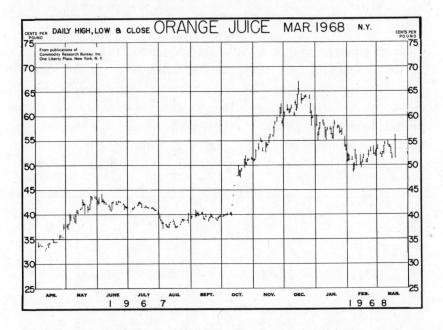

A huge Pork Belly downside breakaway gap in May of 1972 was fully contained within a top area. Yet, there was little doubt as to the destiny of the ensuing trend. Note the small downside breakaway gap in late January that took six weeks to fill, and the huge downside exhaustion gap in June of 1971 that took twenty-five weeks to fill.

Cocoa's major long-term bull market, from July to December 1968, was featured by a large October measuring gap. To the best of my knowledge, no one has ever made a distinction between a measuring and a runaway gap. In the context of gaps, the two words are deemed synonymous. It would seem, however, that the two gaps in mid September could only qualify as runaway gaps in contradistinction to the October one which could only qualify as a meas-

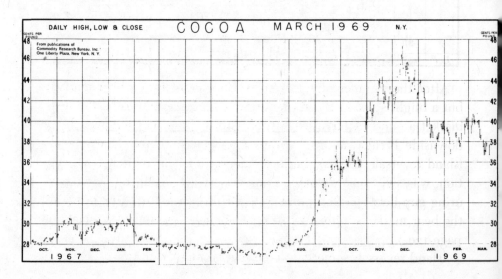

uring gap. Upside breakaway gaps occurred in early September, exhaustion gaps occurred in December, and a downside breakaway gap occurred in January of 1969. Note, also, the classic saucer bottom that preceded this bull market. The only thing missing was a handle.

A downside exhaustion gap, in September of 1971, signaled the end of the major maxi-term bear market that had begun in Silver in the spring of 1968. The bear market, however, had another 20¢ to run. Although the gap has been filled, overhead resistance kept this market dawdling for about one year.

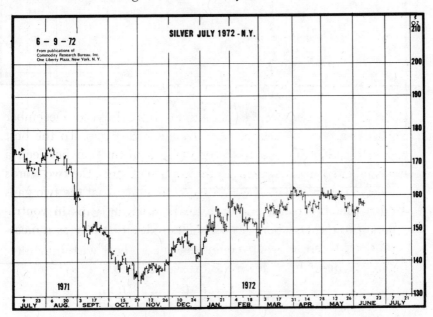

After the summer blight of 1970, Corn went into a bear market; but a blight scare in the spring of 1971 temporarily turned the bear market around. A large exhaustion gap in June was followed by a downside breakaway gap within two weeks, thereby forming an island reversal. The ensuing bear market, or bear market continuation, was swift and virtually a one-way street. Note the July measuring gap between $1.45 and $1.44. This gap occurred precisely at the bear market's midway point. (The chart referred to appears on page 120.)

Island reversals sometimes take several months to form. The 1966

Soybean island reversal is hardly a textbook example inasmuch as the July upside exhaustion gap was filled shortly thereafter. Notwithstanding, trend followers could have gone short with impunity following the September downside breakaway gap.

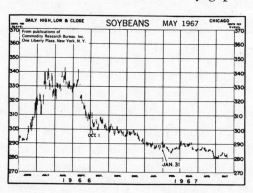

A small downside exhaustion gap in September of 1971 presaged the termination of Cocoa's major maxi-term bear market that had begun in 1969. On precisely the same plane, $24.40, an upside breakaway gap occurred in January of 1972. The island reversal thus formed foretokened firming Cocoa prices.

A one-day island reversal, as already stated, is a rarity. In September 1970, such a reversal occurred in Cocoa. Actually, this island terminated a counter trend to the bear market that had begun in 1969.

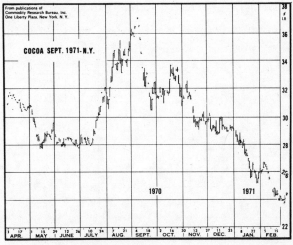

In January 1971, for the first time in almost seven years, the price of Sugar rose above 5¢. Within two months, however, it was again headed below 4¢. A one-day island reversal in the second week of March beaconed the ultimate retreat.

Two-day island reversals are somewhat more prevalent than the one-day variety, but are still quite scarce. The Korean War sent Sugar soaring. A two-day island reversal started it back to earth.

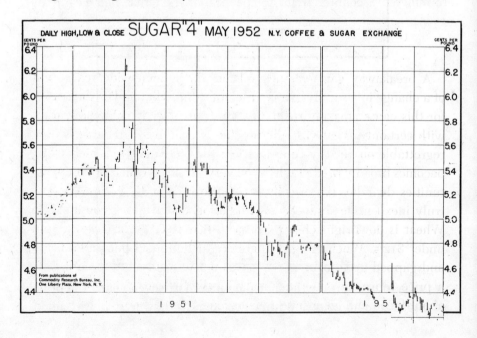

Unique price action triggered a major long-term bull market in 1971 Orange Juice. First came a huge downside exhaustion gap; then an inverted V bottom (a once-in-a-lifetime rarity) and a second downside exhaustion gap; next an upside breakaway gap to form a small island reversal followed by a second upside breakaway gap; and, finally, a third upside breakaway gap to form a large island reversal. Although not shown here, this bull market eventually went above 65¢.

A breakaway gap generally reflects the sudden wide realization of a change in a supply/demand relationship. Therein lies the reason for this clue's amazing reliability. But reliability is not synonymous with certainty. That virtually no clue is ever 100% reliable is only regrettable on cursory consideration, for the extent to which CMA becomes broadly predictable is the very extent to which profit opportunities dwindle. Historically, since World War II, $1.60 Wheat is truly inexpensive. Indeed, with inflation taken into account, $1.60 Wheat is downright cheap. From 1946 to 1964, Wheat never sold under $1.75. When in 1968, therefore, it bottomed out under $1.55 and gapped up to over $1.60, it was not unreasonable to anticipate a price return to more customary levels. Instead, Wheat promptly about-faced and went into a major long-term tailspin.

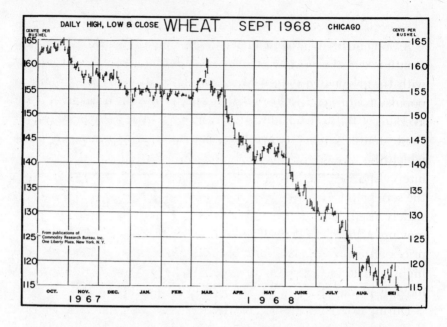

By 1971, Wheat had been in the doghouse for the better part of seven years. Thus, when it gapped up almost 5¢ in June of that year, surely the long-awaited bull market was at hand. Instead, Wheat prices again nosedived—30¢ in two months.

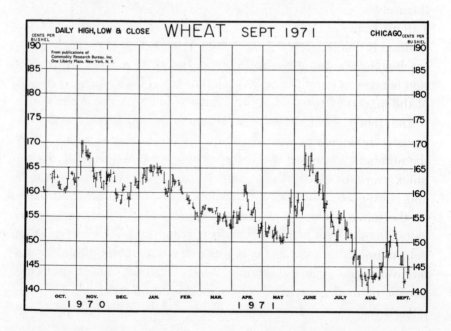

8. *Positioning trends by the moving average method.*

As long as there have been markets, technicians have been experimenting with methods for perceiving and identifying price trends with the purpose of profitably positioning them. One of the more popular traditional methods has been the moving average one. An average is the sum of numerical items divided by the number of those items. A moving average, then, is a progressive average in which the number of items remains constant but, at specified time intervals, a new item is added in replacement of the oldest one in the series. In CMA, 10-day and 20-day moving averages are the most widely used. The shorter the time-span, the more sensitive is the moving average to a trend termination or reversal. Daily closing prices are conventionally employed in the computations with daily highs and lows being frequent adjuncts. Sometimes two different moving average time-spans are used in conjunction with each other.

During extended trend action, prices rise or decline in advance of their attendant moving averages. During such action, a trend is boarded when the advance differential between the price and its moving average (or averages) reaches a minimum predetermined amount or degree. In theory, when the line connecting the moving average computations crosses the line connecting the price moves themselves, thus canceling the advance differential between the two, a trend termination or reversal may be in the offing. The existing position is therefore closed out. When the advance differential again reaches the minimum predetermined amount or degree, a new position is taken. This new position may or may not be on the same side of the market as the prior one.

The more sensitive the moving average and the smaller the amount or degree of the advance differential, the greater will be the number of buy and sell points. Although this seemingly enables quick trend-boarding, it also results in much more whip-sawing and consequent small losses. An illusory benefit of position-taking by the moving average method is that it seems to substitute arithmetical computation for judgment, but it still requires judgment to determine which moving average(s) to use and what advance differential to program for establishing buy and sell points. The chief benefit of moving average position-taking is that it automatically puts its user aboard every trend of substance.

To better perform in your trading account,
Keep watching the changes in volume amount.

10/Volume Action—
Secret of the Pros

Millions of people are continuously watching markets throughout the world, and have been for centuries. Today, housewives, department store buyers, used car dealers, hotel managers, airline executives, and multitudes of others are constantly pricing items for which they are "in the market"—or, simply, "shopping." The markets for most items, being scattered, are considered informal in the sense that they enjoy no central locations. Only a few items enjoy formal exchanges—central locations where up-to-the-minute prices are being posted or broadcasted for all interested parties to perceive. Listed securities enjoy such formal exchanges; so also do some commodities; and so also do commodity futures. For any item traded on a formal exchange, there are two essential things that its market action reveals:

1. Price change activity.
2. Volume action.

The clues revealed by price change activity are indisputably important. In conjunction with those clues revealed by volume action, the tales told by price change activity often become crucially more meaningful. Although technicians seem to sense the significance of volume, they have produced precious little in the way of empirical studies or detailed analyses on the subject. Perhaps they wish to keep the secrets to themselves. At any rate, during certain market phases, clues generated by volume action can be vital to solving the market's otherwise unfathomable mysteries. This is especially true with commodity futures.

Volume action may be classified as either:

1. Attendant.
2. Prognostic.

Attendant volume action is action that can generally be anticipated and, therefore, contains virtually no predictive value. Prognostic volume action, on the other hand, usually constitutes a volume *increase* or *decrease* of generally unanticipated substance or suddenness. Such a volume increase or decrease, as implied, contains a decided predictive value. Action wherein a volume increase or decrease is expected but does not materialize is, of course, definitely prognostic.

It was stated in Chapter 8 that, after a substantial rise or decline, price fluctuations initially are apt to be wide and hectic in reflection of the market's struggle to adjust to a new price level, and then will gradually simmer down. Because congestion areas are the terminals of substantial rises and declines, and because high volume is a concomitant of wide and hectic price fluctuations, volume is usually greatest at a congestion area's inception and then will gradually ebb to the area's ultimate breakout point. This is particularly true with triangle, wedge, pennant, flag, and platform formations. Mid-platform breakouts, however, are normally accompanied by temporary pick-ups in volume. A similar declining tendency is characteristic of volume action in multiple V-shape formations if the peaks or inverted peaks are exclusively considered. In a double top or bottom, there will be greater volume at the first peak than at the second one. The same broad criterion applies to the head and shoulders formation. The left shoulder will enjoy the most volume and the right shoulder the least, with the volume at the head falling somewhere between the two. Inter-peak volume action is customarily light and meaningless. The notable exceptions to the declining volume tendency are the saucer and scallop. Here, volume reaches its low ebb at the nadir or apex. The volume action described in this paragraph is typically attendant because its perception, apart from all other considerations, would in no way help one foresee the direction of the trend that must ultimately emerge from a congestion area in which the subject action was taking place.

However, it was also stated in Chapter 8: ". . . if heavier volume tends to occur toward the lower level of a congestion area in its latter stage of formation, the implication is that important buying support is being given the market and that the next trend will thus be up; and if heavier volume tends to occur toward the upper level, the implication is that important selling pressure is being exerted on the market and that the next trend will thus be down." At first blush, this premise seems to contradict common sense. Actually, it only contradicts inclinations bred from emotions.

First, visualize a commodity fluctuating between 20¢ and 22¢ with its activity accelerating each time 20¢ is approached but slowing to a crawl each time 22¢ draws near. Does that activity at 20¢ seem a bit scary—as if the bottom were about to drop out? And does that lack of activity at 22¢ seem discouraging—as if the commodity had not a friend (or bull) in the world? If these are your reactions, you are being influenced by emotions rather than by logic. In reality, all that activity at 20¢ constitutes an outward expression of friendship in support of the commodity at a price below which it is not likely to go by reason of those friends waiting there to buy it; and that lack of activity at 22¢ is in large part prompted by a concern that aggressive buying there will induce some ill-advised bears to grab tighter onto their dwindling supplies.

Next, visualize the converse of the prior illustration—a commodity fluctuating between 20¢ and 22¢ but with its activity accelerating each time 22¢ is approached and slowing to a crawl each time 20¢ draws near. Does that activity at 22¢ excite you into believing the commodity is about to be launched into an upward swirl? And does that lack of activity at 20¢ seem encouraging? How often have you heard these siren words? "Well, yes, the market was down; but there was no volume." If once again these are your reactions, then once again you are being influenced by emotions rather than by logic. All that activity at 22¢ represents eager sellers. "But," you ask, "how about all those 22¢ buyers?" They are clearly outnumbered or else the market would not back away from that price after such competitive activity. Finally, the bears' reluctance to sell as aggressively at 20¢ is prompted by two reasons: 1. The price isn't as right. 2. They don't want to scare away the buyers; or, in colloquial terms, they don't want to rock the boat.

The foregoing volume action is typically prognostic. Indeed, clues generated by such action are especially valuable to those who are alert to them, because there are so few who do perceive them when they occur. It's a rare head and shoulders that is overlooked by the fraternity of technicians, but volume action is seldom given more than casual notice by even the most diligent CMA followers. The greater the following, the less golden the opportunity. Conversely, the smaller the following, the more golden the opportunity.

However, relying exclusively on volume may at times be confusing, or even misleading. Let us suppose that, following a rally from 20¢ to 22¢, a burst of 2000 contracts within a day promptly sends the price of a commodity back down to 20¢. There it dawdles for two weeks at a 300-contract-per-day pace. Is this action bullish or bearish? The 2000 contract burst of volume at 22¢ was clearly bearish; but the ability of the market to absorb 3000 contracts at 20¢, albeit over a period of 10 days, must certainly be regarded as offsettingly bullish to some extent. A point and figure chart, by disclosing the price change activity at each price level, might very well solve the dilemma. Just this sort of commonplace situation should encourage technicians to follow both vertical line and point and figure charts.

Breakout points constitute one of the most deceptive phases of CMA. One reason is that a breakout point often cannot be objectively determined. Another reason is that so many breakouts end up by being false ones or traps. As a consequence, to be of prognostic value at these CMA junctures, volume action should be considered together with congestion area analysis and the commodity's location in its historical price range.

After a congestion area has prevailed long enough to be widely recognized and easily delineated, large numbers of buyers and sellers usually will have accumulated in the wings ready to jump into the market each time the congestion area's lower and upper limits are approached. Consequently, for a downside breakout to eventuate, many buyers will have to be satisfied; and, for an upside breakout to eventuate, much selling will have to be absorbed. In either case, the result will be a marked pick-up in trading activity. Since such would be generally expected, this volume action has no prognostic value and must therefore be labelled attendant. Thus, the customary marked pick-up in trading activity after a breakout leaves the validity of that breakout in doubt. Is there enough enthusiasm in support of the nascent trend to absorb the volume? Only time will tell. If the volume subsides and the trend proceeds on its way, then the breakout was indeed valid. But if the volume remains high and the trend promptly reverses itself, then the breakout's validity will continue to be left in doubt. In the latter event, two other possibilities remain:

1. If the trend materially penetrates the congestion area from which it just priorly emerged, the trend should be abandoned —at least for the time being.
2. On the other hand, if the trend again reverses itself by smartly bouncing off the outer range of the subject congestion area, then the trend should be followed with enthusiasm.

It is when the expected pick-up in volume does not materialize at a breakout point that the action becomes immediately prognostic. This infrequent circumstance invariably occurs in a market which has temporarily lost its speculative following. When there are but few speculators around to relieve the trade[1] of its risks, the fabrication of a false breakout would be tantamount to setting a mouse trap in an igloo. Therefore, such a breakout may be followed with confidence and enthusiasm.

During trend action, volume action is normally attendant. A market advances; then retraces part of its advance; advances to a new high; and again partially retraces its most recent advance. Or, a

[1] Refer to Chapter 2, footnotes 11 & 17.

market declines; then retraces part of its decline; declines to a new low; and again partially retraces its most recent decline. Whichever, the volume escorting the overall trends will be greater than the volume escorting the counter trends.

Within the context of overall trend action are four categories of minor turning points; or, simply, minor reversals:

1. Overall uptrend reverts into counter downtrend.
2. Counter downtrend reverts back into overall uptrend.
3. Overall downtrend reverts into counter uptrend.
4. Counter uptrend reverts back into overall downtrend.

Unless there is a noticeable increase or decrease in volume at such a juncture, volume by itself will be of no prognostic value. Again, a point and figure chart might help. Fortunately, however, noticeable volume increases or decreases frequently attend these reversals. On balance, overall trend reversions into counter trends (as per examples 1 and 3) are attended by volume dry-ups while counter trend reversions back into overall trends (as per examples 2 and 4) are attended by volume pick-ups. The reason is that buyers dominate and are thereby more aggressive during overall uptrends whereas sellers dominate and are thereby more aggressive during overall downtrends. Consequently, when buyers temporarily shift from aggressiveness to patience in an overall uptrend, volume will dry up and the market will then recede. Conversely, when sellers temporarily shift from aggressiveness to patience in an overall downtrend, volume will dry up and the market will then rally. Consequently, also, when buyers recommence their aggressiveness in an overall uptrend, volume will pick up and the market will then resume its advance. And, conversely, when sellers recommence their aggressiveness in an overall downtrend, volume will pick up and the market will then resume its decline.

There are two types of market reversals, minor and major. As we have seen, a minor reversal is the conversion of an overall trend into a counter trend, or vice versa. A major reversal, however, is the conversion of an overall uptrend into an overall downtrend, or vice versa. A minor reversal may constitute or be part of an area of re-accumulation or an area of re-distribution, or may be neither.

A major reversal, on the other hand, is always a bottom or a top.

Of all CMA phases, the perception of volume action during major reversals is most crucial to trading success. The volume action during the stock market tops of 1929, 1937, 1946, 1962, 1966, and 1969 clearly prophesied imminent bear markets. Any who lost their shirts in these markets were clearly blind to the volume action at those major reversal junctures. As implied, the perception of volume action is somewhat more valuable at stock market tops than at stock market bottoms. The same implication is true for individual stocks. It is also true for individual commodities. The reason is as follows:

Volume action during major reversals forecasts two things:

1. That the prevailing overall trend is nearing an end or has ended.
2. That the next overall trend will be in the opposite direction.

Because the duration of tops is normally so much briefer than the duration of bottoms, it is far easier to be trapped into the wrong side of a market within its top region than within its bottom region. For the same reason, it takes far greater mental agility to go short a market at its top than to go long a market at its bottom. Of course, market tops are potentially more treacherous than market bottoms for another quite obvious reason: Human nature is more bullishly than bearishly inclined.

After a commodity has enjoyed an extended price advance on steady volume or steadily increasing volume, a point of time will come when a final contingent of obstinate shorts will begin to hasten toward the exit at a panic rate of intensity. They will be joined by others eager to get on the long side of the bandwagon before the parade is entirely over. The result will be abnormally high volume along with wide and hectic price fluctuations. The newly elevated price level may linger for a while, or may go even higher. Volume may stay high, or may gradually diminish. Regardless of these secondary characteristics, the initial message remains crystal-clear: "The bull market is over."

Diabolically, abnormally high volume along with wide and hectic price fluctuations after an extended price advance exudes a bullish aura. However, remember that for each contract traded, half that trade constitutes a sale. To the point: Seasoned traders do not get fooled by such an aura; and, on the boardroom stage, cheers are echoed by bulls while the smart action is being unobtrusively taken by the bears.

High volume along with wide and hectic price fluctuations after an extended price advance is known as an upside volume blowoff. Downside volume blowoffs are as common but not usually as pronounced nor as easy to identify. By reason of the bullish inclination of human nature, downside volume blowoffs are frequently imagined long before they actually occur. Customarily, therefore, a series of alleged volume blowoffs will precede the valid volume blowoff that signals the end of a bear market. Volume blowoffs of less dramatic substance may also signal the termination of lengthy counter trends.

To confuse things a bit, volume dry-ups at times signal the termination of counter trends. After a counter downtrend has run its course, for example, there may come a period of time when the volume action is so quiet that a pall seems to have settled over the market. This simply means the selling pressure is off and would-be buyers are exerting restraint. Such restraint is usually prompted by the knowledge of offerings so thin that big bids will go largely unsated and aggressive competitive bids will send prices spiraling. At any rate, these quiet periods are generally splendid opportunities to buy the market with the converse, of course, being true after a counter uptrend has run its course.

A popular phenomenon with technicians is the *period of time price reversal*. This period ordinarily covers one day, sometimes one week, and occasionally one month. An upside daily reversal would be a day on which a price opened higher than the prior session's closing price but then closed, that same day, lower than the prior session's closing price. Upside weekly and monthly reversals, and downside reversals, are all definitionally self-evident.

An upside reversal within a bottom is virtually meaningless. An upside reversal within a prevailing uptrend may foreshadow a counter downtrend. An upside reversal within a counter uptrend or an area of re-distribution quite likely foreshadows a continuation of the prevailing overall downtrend. An upside reversal within a suspected top formation should add confirmation to one's suspicions. Lastly, but most importantly, an upside reversal attended by unusually high volume should be taken much more seriously than one attended by normal volume. The converse, again of course, would be true for downside reversals.

The intra-day volume action of a commodity often conforms to a pattern. For a commodity with a sizable speculative following, the common volume pattern is heavier volume during the opening and closing minutes of trading with fairly uniform activity in between. Such a pattern offers many profitable scalping opportunities as well as frequently enabling one to enter markets at opportune times.

If a market opens higher on pretty heavy volume, usually the market will then settle back for a while. Conversely, if a market opens lower on pretty heavy volume, usually the market will then firm up for a while. The reason is that pretty heavy opening volume is largely reflective of accumulated overnight orders stimulated by factors already widely known.

In the context of the aforegoing volume action pattern, there are two types of higher or lower closings:

1. Where prices continue to rise or fall right up to the close.
2. Where prices stop rising or falling in roughly the last 15 minutes to an hour of trading, but during this time fluctuate and remain at or near their highs or lows of the day.

In example 1, where prices continue to rise right up to the close, a higher opening may be anticipated the following trading day. Conversely, where prices continue to fall right up to the close, a lower opening may be anticipated the following trading day. In example 2, on the other hand, the reverse may be anticipated. After an up day with prices stalled on pretty heavy volume in the last half hour or so, supply has caught up with demand and lower prices may be anticipated at the next session's opening. Conversely, after a down day with prices holding on pretty heavy volume in the last half hour or so, demand has caught up with supply and higher prices may be anticipated at the next session's opening.

The relationship between unusually high volume and normal volume varies from commodity to commodity, and varies from time to time with respect to the same commodity. The greater the continuous speculative following enjoyed by a commodity, the less will be the differential between its high and normal volume days. With Pork Belly contracts, which enjoy a continuous speculative following, high volume days generally run no more than 50% greater than normal volume days. With Hog contracts, which do not enjoy a continuous speculative following, high volume days will generally run at least 100% greater than normal volume days.

In CMA, it is sometimes advisable to appraise volume action as it relates to *open interest*: the outstanding contractual commitments into which traders have entered. For example, let us suppose that the volume in a commodity with an open interest of 10,000 contracts normally runs 2,000 contracts per day. A 4,000 contract volume day would then be considered a high volume one. But, were the open interest of that commodity to climb to 20,000 contracts over a period of time, then a 4,000 contract volume day would be considered just normal.

Open interest varies from day to day as new contractual commitments are entered into and old ones are liquidated. Most open interest increases and decreases are nominal. When open interest climbs or falls sharply, however, then it may be important to consider it as a clue by itself.

As with volume, open interest ordinarily climbs during bull markets and falls during bear markets. If during a bull market there is an inordinate increase in open interest, the end of that bull market might well be at hand. Conversely, if during a bear market there is an inordinate decrease in open interest, the end of that bear market might well be at hand.

After a price rise, a congestion area may be either an area of re-accumulation or a top. If open interest continues to climb while prices start leveling off, a top should be suspected. After a price decline, a congestion area either may be an area of re-distribution or a bottom. If open interest continues to be liquidated while prices are leveling off, a bottom should be suspected. In the first instance, the bulls' domination was being effectively challenged by new selling. In the second instance, the bears' domination was being effectively challenged by new buying.

Sometimes, during a market rise, there will be a sudden reduction in open interest. Under this circumstance, one may conclude that the market is being dominated by short covering. Such a market is generally considered technically weak, at least for the time being.

With some commodities, open interest is known to vary seasonally. In those cases where the seasonal variation is significant, it is important to be knowledgeable of same for reasons which now should be self-evident. For instance, Pork Belly open interest normally peaks at the end of December or at the beginning of January and then diminishes as it approaches the end of its crop year— reaching its lowest point with the final liquidation of the August contract. It then of course climbs until the turn of the calendar year. In August and September, a volume of 8,000 contracts is considered high for Bellies. In January and February, the same volume would be considered low. These figures will change as speculative interest in Belly contracts vacillates. Hog and Pork Belly open interest seasonal patterns run roughly parallel.

The liquidation of the May futures contract signals the end of the Potato crop year. From that point of time, Potato open interest climbs until February and then comes under liquidation. With the grains and their allied products, open interest is normally lowest in the spring and greatest during the fall harvesting season. Egg open interest reaches its peak toward the end of summer and its nadir during winter.

Cattle and Sugar come to market in fairly even quantities throughout the year and are therefore not subject to open interest seasonal variation patterns. Although Cocoa, Orange Juice, and Cotton are crop-year products, the sporadic speculative enthusiasm in them has distorted their open interest seasonal patterns to the point where they are of little significance. This may change, particularly with respect to Cotton. Should the revival of speculation in Cotton be sustained on a relatively continuous basis, its open interest pattern may eventually assume crop-year characteristics. It is still too early to know whether or not Plywood and Lumber open interest will vary seasonally.

One would not expect Silver, Copper, and Platinum to be subject to open interest seasonal variation. But they are. In the three or four months prior to the end of the calendar year, the open interest perceptibly picks up in these three metals, especially in Silver. Then suddenly, in the first week of January, the open interest of each comes under substantial liquidation. The reason is tax straddles which will be the principal topic of the next chapter.

"The economic facts of life are many. But the grandfather of them all is the law of demand and supply."[1] With chagrin, I must admit that this law is temporarily repealed during all emotionally fueled bull and bear markets. What initially signals the law's repeal? Volume action. The law, however, does not long remain repealed. What signals its return as a potent market force? Again, volume action. On the surface, volume action, like the temporary repeal of the law of demand and supply, may seem capricious. It is not. There is a reason for everything. To locate a reason, one's best resource is his own logic. This is especially true of volume action—because so little has been written about it.

---

[1] Anthony M. Reinach, *The First Law of Economics*, Essays on Liberty, Volume IV, The Foundation for Economic Education, 1958, page 38.

The Law of Gravity
Has almost no laxation.
One noted oddity
Is government taxation.

11/Taxes and Commodity Futures

If there were a business of arbitraging currencies in the West Indies, whatever that means, most of us would understandably assume that such a business was realizing huge profits and paying precious little in the way of taxes on them. Strangely, many regard commodity trading in much the same light. It is not true. Commodity profits are not easy to come by, and those earned are ineradicably recorded on brokerage house statements which are subject to close scrutiny by the IRS.

Furthermore, whereas ordinary business losses can be used as an offset against prior or future years' profits or against other current income, trading losses in commodity futures enjoy no such luxury. Trading losses in commodity futures are capital losses. As such, they cannot be used to offset prior years' trading profits, or current income beyond $1,000. Other than that $1,000 of current income, they can only be used to offset capital gains earned in the current year, or be carried forward to offset future capital gains that may or may not materialize. Consequently, except for profits he can carry forward into a subsequent year, a commodity trader cannot boast the same cushions with which other businessmen are endowed. For him, each new year is virtually a new ball game. The only tax benefit a commodity trader does have is the one he shares with all other sufferers of capital losses, namely: He can carry forward those losses for the rest of his life or as long as they exist.

Commodity futures, however, do provide a vehicle whereby *any* individual can seek to achieve two tax-saving goals:

1. He can try to defer taxes on short-term capital gains from one year to the next, and even for his entire life. He can also try to defer taxes on long-term capital gains, but here it is highly questionable as to whether the end result will be profitable.
2. He can try to convert short-term capital gains into long-term capital gains.

Unless one is able to defer taxes on short-term capital gains until after death, at which time the gain will be merely subject to an inheritance tax, the deferment rarely constitutes a tax saving. Most often, it simply postpones the payment of taxes for a period of time during which the individual retains the use of money he would have otherwise paid the government.

There is one set of circumstances under which a taxpayer actually achieves a tax saving by shelving a short-term capital gains liability for a year. For instance:

1. In 1973, taxpayer realizes a net $25,000 of short-term capital gains that is deferred to 1974.
2. In 1974, taxpayer realizes a net $25,000 of short-term capital losses. This offsets his carried-forward gains, so no tax is paid on those gains.

Had the taxpayer not deferred his 1973 gains, he would have paid on them a tax that can never really be fully recovered. In the first place, he necessarily loses an incalculable use of money. In the second place, he must either realize gains in subsequent years against which the losses may be offset, or he must live 25 years to employ the losses against ordinary income at the rate of $1,000 per year, or a combination thereof. Thus, in view of the 1974 loss, the deferment of the 1973 gain must be regarded as indeed profitable.

The vehicle which offers the aforementioned tax-saving goals is the tax straddle. Happily, the futures trading novice with a short-term capital gains problem can employ commodity tax straddles with practically no chance of serious loss and with a very good chance of achieving his goals. Silver futures contracts traded on the New York Commodity Exchange are not only ideal for purposes of illustration, they are also by far the most popular vehicle for tax straddling. The reasons are threefold:

1. These contracts are extremely liquid.
2. Silver is highly volatile.
3. The New York Commodity Exchange floor brokers are very cooperative in accommodating tax straddlers.

The contract months for which there is Silver trading are:

January	July
March	September
May	December

Let us now suppose that the month is August or September, that an individual has realized a net $10,000 of short-term capital gains in the current year, and that he will be faced with a $6,000 tax liability should he do nothing about these gains. Putting on tax straddles in Silver may at least shelve his tax liability for a year and thereby acquire for him an additional year's use of the money he would have otherwise remitted to the government. Since Silver usually rises or declines 10¢ or more at least once within most three-month periods of time, and since a 1¢ move in Silver represents a $100 fluctuation per contract, a 10-straddle position would be recommended for the attempted deferral of $10,000 of short-term capital gains. A suggested *straight* straddle position would be either to go short 10 January contracts and to go long 10 March contracts, or vice versa.

It would be truly convenient if Silver were to achieve a 10¢ rise or decline in precise coincidence with the end of the calendar year. Then the taxpayer could simply liquidate the loss side of his position on the last day of the current year and the profit side on the first day of the new year and take his chances with a leg lifted over night. This, however, is not what customarily transpires. Generally, Silver will have achieved a 10¢ move somewhat before the last trading day in December. Now the taxpayer is confronted with this decision: Should he maintain his straddle position in the hope that the move will be sustained, or should he quickly establish the loss side of his straddle—now that his goal has been reached?

To establish his loss is the obvious prudent course of action, for not to do so would risk the dissolution of his already attained goal. But this raises a still further problem: What to do about the lifted leg? As a case in point, suppose the taxpayer had sold 10 Januaries and had bought 10 Marches, and that the market is down 10¢ by the middle of November, thereby creating an unrealized $10,000 profit in the January contracts and an unrealized $10,000 loss in the March contracts. To liquidate the 10 Marches will establish the desired $10,000 short-term capital loss, but will also leave the taxpayer short 10 Januaries with no protection. To provide the required protection, 10 Mays are purchased simultaneously with the liquidation of the 10 Marches.

There are price differentials between the various open contract months. These are known as *spreads*. Spreads in Silver usually remain quite constant, but can materially change. A *butterfly* tax straddle virtually eliminates the risk of spread changes. A suggested butterfly straddle position would be to go long 10 Mays and to go short 5 Januaries and 5 Septembers. Should the market decline 10¢, the 10 long Mays would be liquidated and replaced by 5 long Marches and 5 long Julys. Should the market rise 10¢, the 5 short Januaries and 5 short Septembers would be liquidated and replaced by 5 short Marches and 5 short Julys. Where the objective is exclusively the deferment of a tax liability, there is no purpose in not liquidating the final position on the first trading day in January.

Straight or butterfly straddles are essentially 3-step operations. In Silver, the pre-tax cost roughly approximates $100 per straddle, or $1,000 for a 10-straddle operation. Thus, the realization of a $10,000 short-term capital loss in one year will result in the realization of about a $9,000 short-term capital gain in the following year. For a Silver straddle, the current margin requirement is $300, or $3,000 for 10 straddles. Computed in the overall cost of a straddle opera-tion must be the loss of the use of the money required for margin. Obviously, the fewer the straddles used to achieve an objective, the lower will be that achievement's cost. Analogously, though, the fewer the straddles used, the less likely will be the complete fulfill-ment of the desired objective.

The benefit derived from carrying forward short-term capital gains is quite psychological. It enables one to begin the new year with short-term capital gains. Against these, one can more freely take risks in the knowledge that corresponding losses will be largely government sustained. But combining the deferment of short-term capital gains with taking a shot at converting them into long-term capital gains makes considerably more financial sense.

A suggested procedure for accomplishing this double objective would be, in the month of August, to sell March Silver and buy May Silver. Should the price of Silver rise 10¢ before the end of the year, March Silver should be covered to establish the desired loss and simultaneously replaced by a sale of July Silver. If the market rise dissolves before the Mays are 6 months old, then the entire remaining position should be liquidated within 5 months and 29 days. On the other hand, if the market rise is to some extent sustained beyond 6 months, the position should be liquidated soon after the long-term period has been established. If the straddler thinks Silver is going even higher and wishes to play for additional long-term gains, he may immediately replace his liquidated straddles with new ones—using contract months of the following year. Unless the rise at the time of liquidation is precisely 10¢, there will be left over either a short-term capital gain or a short-term capital loss from the July position. If desired, this gain or loss can be carried forward by putting on new straddles later in the current year.

An interesting opportunity presents itself when Silver declines 10¢ before the end of the year in which the initial straddles were put on. In this event, May Silver should be sold to establish the de-sired loss and simultaneously replaced by a purchase of July Silver. Now should Silver prices turn around and recover, the straddler will have a shot at a long-term capital gain in a market that initially seemed to behave in recalcitrance to his long-term capital gain objective.

Although Silver has been dramatized as the optimum vehicle for tax straddles, other commodities frequently provide far superior opportunities to convert short-term gains into long-term ones. If the straddler thinks Silver prices are destined to remain in the doldrums over the foreseeable future, then he should by all means search out a commodity whose prospects are more to his liking. Even in the selection of tax straddles, there is no substitute for individual judgment. Before adopting any tax straddle program, however, one would be well advised to consult his accountant or tax adviser.

There's one wisdom that will last:
Man learns nothing from the past!

12/Money Action—
or the Inflation Game

Recently, ten foreign currency futures began trading on the Chicago Mercantile Exchange and on the International Commercial Exchange in New York. Why? Because the value relationships between these currencies, and between them and the dollar, are being so perseveringly altered by inflation on a continuing basis that currency futures have become recognized as potentially excellent trading vehicles.

Inflation is the peaceful procedure that enables government to acquire its citizens' wealth without having to tax or borrow it. For some 2600 years, since the birth of modern money, inflation has been a way of life throughout the civilized areas of the world. The one

[1] Portions of this chapter were abstracted from: Anthony M. Reinach, "Demand Deposit Inflation," *The Freeman*, The Foundation for Economic Education, January 1968.

major notable exception was the United States for the first 160 years of its history. For over a century prior to World War II, the commodity price level in the United States had not materially risen except *temporarily* during the Civil War and during World War I. Since the beginning of World War II, however, the commodity price level in the United States has *permanently* more than doubled. Why? Because America, too, has adopted inflation as a way of life.

To be able to visualize what's in store for the commodity markets, one has to understand inflation; and to understand inflation, one has to understand money.

Money is like sex in one respect. Most people understand it, but not too well. The initial problem with money is semantic. Unlike any other term in the English language, so far as I know, the term money identifies two different important entities within the same intellectual context.

Take the term *diamond.* In the context of precious gems, it identifies the one of near pure carbon in crystalline form. In the context of baseball, it identifies mainly the infield. In the context of printing, it identifies a small size of type; namely, 4½ point. In the context of playing cards, it identifies a particular suit. And, in the context of anniversaries, it identifies the sixtieth. So long as a term identifies no more than one entity in a particular context, there should be no confusion. If, however, in the context of precious gems, the term diamond not only were used to identify the one of near pure carbon in crystalline form, but also were used to identify the one of bright-green transparency, we would often be confused as to whether the reference to diamonds meant diamonds as we know them, or meant emeralds.

Now take the term *money.* Those paper bills and coins in your purse or wallet are tools of exchange, which are money. But, in the same context, the quantifiers of those tools, dollars and cents, are also money. It's as if the word *scale* were used to identify both weighing equipment and the terms that quantify weight: ounces, pounds, tons, and so forth. Although the close relationship between the two monetary entities may seem to justify the double-duty semantic use of the term money, that double-duty use actually contributes to an umbrella of confusion under which governments are able to play "The Inflation Game" without many citizens' being able to recognize the game's nature and its consequences to them.

Technologically, the money tool has taken four basic forms: raw commodity, coin, paper, and checking account. During those many centuries when raw commodities served as the money tools, taxation was the only fiscal connection between money and government. Inflation thus remained an unknown phenomenon. But, with the emergence of coins, government hungrily eyed the new action. On the admirable premise that its citizens needed protection from counterfeiters, government usurped the coinage of the money tool. With irreverent promptness, government also commandeered its counterfeiting.

Inflation is the euphemism for government counterfeiting. During those centuries that the principal money tool evolved from coin to paper to checking account, inflation collaterally evolved from coin debasement to printing press to the creation of spurious demand deposits (checking account funds). Throughout, government has abided as the sole croupier.

Coin debasement was initiated by the Greeks and later adopted by the Romans. At first, they simply "clipped" the coins and used the fragments to create additional ones. This crude procedure later gave way to the more refined one of "sweating." Here, the precious metal was melted so that part of it could be detached and replaced by a cheaper substance. The precious metal thus detached was then used for additional coinage. The final coin-debasement innovation was supplied by various Chinese governments which kept punching ever bigger holes into the middles of their citizens' money tools. Interestingly, the Chinese were also the forerunners of paper money inflation. That they accomplished this even before the invention of the printing press further establishes the Chinese as people of inscrutable ingenuity.

The French were responsible for two of history's most dramatic paper money explosions, the John Law and the Assignat inflations.

The John Law monetary experiments permanently memorialized the irony that a government will just as eagerly commit an act of knavery as it will eagerly incarcerate a private citizen for committing the very same act. A shivering economic fact is that a government panacea designed to cure or correct a condition will, instead, inevitably further aggravate that condition. The Assignat inflation was no exception. Here, the French government confiscated church real estate to use as backing for her paper money issues. Mesmerized by the fiscal stability such vast holdings should have afforded, the political establishment sharply increased its nation's spending programs. All this was done, of course, for the good of the little people. It was the little people, however, who suffered most from the resultant dire economic conditions that ushered in the Napoleonic Era. As with the Assignat inflation, virtually every other monetary inflation throughout history most victimized those it was most supposed to help, with perhaps one exception. Post World War I Germany deliberately embarked on an inflationary policy to relieve her citizens of the yoke attributed to reparations. Although the policy was a surface success, the rewards were too meager or too short-lived to keep that nation from seeking a Hitler to cure, among other things, those conditions inflation had failed to ultimately alleviate.

Bankers, banks, and bank credit money are known to have existed in ancient Babylon. Modern banking probably began in 16th-century Venice. The evolution of modern banking has been paralleled by the evolution of bank credit money—also known as check money, checking account funds, and demand deposits. But the evolution was slow. As recently as the 19th century, currency remained man's principal tool of exchange. It wasn't until after World War I that demand deposits clearly took over first place. Today, in America, demand deposits are the tools in over 90% of our exchanges.

The ascendancy of private bank money saw government finding itself increasingly hard-pressed to play the inflation game with its customary success. There was only one solution: Government, too, would have to engage in the banking business. In some countries, governments started their own. In other countries, governments nationalized those of their citizens. Thanks to Andrew Jackson, only in America was government barred from the banking business—albeit for less than a century.

In Europe, a government-owned bank is euphemistically known as a "central" bank. In America, it is affectionately referred to as the "Fed." With banks of their own, governments were back in the inflation game with a vengeance. The modern name of the game, of course, is demand deposit inflation. If private citizens enjoyed the same playing rights, the game would go something like this:

Imagine yourself in the role of a drugstore owner. The name of your drugstore is Fiscal Pharmacy, and you operate it with one employee, Samuel. You wish to remodel your drugstore at a cost of $10,000, but all your funds are being used for other purposes and you have already stretched your credit to just about the last penny. It seems that you will have to abandon, or at least postpone, your remodeling program. But then you get an idea!

You go to your local printer and instruct him to print up $10,000 worth of 30-year bonds on Fiscal Pharmacy, to yield 3½ per cent. In addition, you instruct your printer to make up a checkbook for "The Samuel Trust Company." A few days later, armed with the freshly printed bonds and checkbook, you summon Samuel to inform him of a proprietary position with which you are about to reward him for his loyalty:

YOU: I have decided to remodel Fiscal Pharmacy. It will take $10,000.

SAMUEL: That's a lot of potatoes.

YOU: Yes, and I haven't been able to raise the first dollar.

SAMUEL: Maybe you should cut your personal living expenses.

YOU: And have my wife throw me out?

SAMUEL: So what do you propose?

YOU: Here's my plan. From now on, you will function not only as a clerk, but also as the private banker for Fiscal Pharmacy.

SAMUEL: But I haven't got $10,000.

YOU: You won't need it. In fact, you won't need any of it.

SAMUEL: No?

YOU: No. Here's $10,000 worth of bonds on Fiscal Pharmacy and a checkbook for "The Samuel Trust Company." Your bank now owns the bonds, so please pay for them by issuing to Fiscal Pharmacy a check in the amount of $10,000.

On the hypothetical assumption that the banking system must extend to private citizens the same courtesies it extends to government, you deposit the $10,000 check with an established commercial bank and thereby create the wherewithal for your remodeling program. The funds you subsequently transfer to your decorator and contractor will soon be transferred by them to their own creditors and others, and so forth. Thus begins the process by which the $10,000 you and Samuel conspired to create become diffused throughout the country's entire commercial banking system.

Fictitious? Yes. Fantastic? No. The conspiratorial procedure by which you and Samuel created the initial bogus $10,000 is the essence of the manner in which governments, today, trigger monetary inflation.

If the impact on the nation's money supply were simply an added $10,000, the harm done might not be worth analyzing. But, because commercial banks in the United States are permitted by law to lend out roughly 80 per cent of their deposits, and because these banks since World War II have been vigorously lending out virtually every dollar allowed by law, an additional $8,000 (80 per cent of $10,000) of loans, or investments in credit instruments, will be promptly made. These new loans will be just as promptly returned to the banking system as new demand deposits and will, in turn, enable the banks to lend out another $6,400 (80 per cent of $8,000), which will likewise be deposited and generate the additional lending of $5,120, et cetera, et cetera, et cetera. The final result will be $40,000 of additional or derivative demand deposits spawned from the initial bogus $10,000 demand deposit for a grand total of $50,000. In the USA, how newly created money mushrooms into five times its original amount is not even privileged information; indeed, it is publicized by the government iself.

In any country with a modern fiscal set-up, monetary inflation begins with that country's Federal budget. To meet its budget, a government can tax, borrow, or inflate. It's when taxation and borrowing fail to raise the desired funds that inflation is resorted to.

Essentially, there are two game plans for inflating demand deposits. These game plans may be categorized as:

1. Demand deposit inflation European style.
2. Demand deposit inflation American style.

Because demand deposit inflation European style is the less complex of the two, let's first observe it in action:

Take an imaginary European country with a $50 billion federal budget. Now suppose the government of this country taxes $40 billion and borrows $8 billion, still leaving it $2 billion short. At this point, its Treasury would enter in the role of Fiscal Pharmacy's owner, and its Central Bank would enter in the role of Samuel, the captive private banker.

EUROPEAN TREASURY: Our expenses this year are $50 billion.

CENTRAL BANK: That's a lot of potatoes.

EUROPEAN TREASURY: We were able to tax only $40 billion.

CENTRAL BANK: Maybe you should cut expenses, or raise taxes by 20 per cent.

EUROPEAN TREASURY: And get thrown out of office? (In South America, where the inflation game is played with unparalleled gusto, the word *assassinated* would be used instead of the words *thrown out of office.*)

CENTRAL BANK: Well, how much were you able to borrow?

EUROPEAN TREASURY: $8 billion.

CENTRAL BANK: That still leaves you $2 billion short.

EUROPEAN TREASURY: Yes, so here's $2 billion worth of bonds. Please pay me for them.

To get such funds honored by the banking system required a hypothetical assumption in the case of Fiscal Pharmacy. Needless to say, no hypothetical assumption is required here.

In the USA, the process begins in much the same manner—down to the final step, that is:

AMERICAN TREASURY: Our expenses this year are $250 billion.

FED: That's a lot of potatoes.

AMERICAN TREASURY: We were able to tax only $200 billion.

FED: Maybe you should cut expenses, or raise taxes by 20 per cent.

AMERICAN TREASURY: And get voted out of office?

FED: Well, how much were you able to borrow?

AMERICAN TREASURY: $40 billion.

FED: That still leaves you $10 billion short.

At this juncture, the American game plan departs from the European in that the freshly printed bonds will not be sold directly to the Fed, but will instead be peddled in the so-called money market. Does that mean the Fed is going to be allowed to stay off the hook? Only if the money market can absorb the issues without becoming unsettled. Otherwise, before these bonds are peddled, the Fed will be notified of the situation and "persuaded" to buy *other* bonds in the money market with the exclusive purpose of creating the very market-place climate required by the Treasury to dispose of its own. The final result, however, will be the same as if the Treasury had sold the bonds directly to the Fed in the first place. In fact, the net result may be even more inflationary, for it is quite possible that the Fed might have to buy $11 billion worth of bonds in the market to enable the Treasury to dispose of its $10 billion. Remember— each $1 billion worth of bonds purchased by the Fed spawns $5 billion of additional demand deposits throughout the commercial banking system.

Of course, this process does not take place all at one time. Prior to World War II, the Fed actually owned fewer than $5 billion of government bonds. During World War II, the Fed accumulated an additional $20 billion. Then, for fourteen years, the Fed's portfolio remained fairly stable. But, from 1960 to 1972, the Fed's ownership of government bonds increased from $26 billion to over $70 billion, and *that* is the root cause of today's inflation.

Demand deposit inflation American style, truly a monument to Yankee ingenuity, owes its vitality to what is known as *open market operations*. Open market operations are simply the buying and selling of government bonds by the Fed. The Fed's purpose in buying government bonds, as we have seen, is generally to maintain or create a climate in which the Treasury can sell its own without unduly shaking up the money market. In theory, after the Treasury is rid of its current offerings, the Fed is supposed to turn around and merchandise its own recent purchases. In practice, sad to relate, the Fed is rarely able to more than partially accomplish this. For one thing, the Treasury is rarely without bonds for sale. For another thing, the aggressive unloading of bonds by the Fed would drive up interest rates to allegedly intolerable levels.

The game plan for inflation also includes such strategies as *reserve requirements* and the *rediscount rate*. As with the semantics of money, these strategies help disguise the naked nature of the overall game plan. By increasing checking account funds, inflation simply reduces the value of that which quantifies them—the dollar. Correspondingly, within twenty years, inflation will make worth a million dollars much property that today is perhaps worth but $500,000. It's like tinkering with the length of a foot ruler. Shortening it would make us all six-footers, and elongating it would make us all pygmies. Or would it?

A clipped coin, or a coin through which a hole has been punched, is easy to recognize. A coin from which a portion of the precious metal has been detached through sweating and replaced by a cheaper substance will either weigh less or take on a different appearance. A sudden increase in paper money may take longer to recognize, but not too much longer. An increase in demand deposits, however, is the most unrecognizable inflation of them all, because a demand deposit is not a physical entity. It cannot be perceived by any of the five senses. It is exclusively represented by a bookkeeping entry. But the Fed's ownership of government bonds can be closely followed; and so long as such ownership keeps on increasing, so also will all extant price levels.

There is only one way inflation can be halted. That way is balanced federal budgets. There is absolutely no other way. Unless balanced budgets are in the offing, the prices of commodity futures will work persistently higher. Although the various advances will not be without severe setbacks, the former prices of first one commodity and then another will gradually be left behind never to be again seen. By 1985, food prices will be more than double their prices today. In the futures markets, to cite just two commodities, Cotton will be selling for over $1.00 a pound and Silver for over $4.00 an ounce. As a hedge against inflation, why not try commodity futures?

When you decide the price is right
For that which suits you to a tee,
You buy it with a child's delight
And take it home most happily.
　　Nor need you be at all afraid
　　That you, for it, much overpaid;
　　For pleasure is the standard where
　　You buy for future wear and tear.
But buying *future* Corn or Wheat
For what might seem indeed a song
May turn out rather indiscreet
'Cause simply this: The price was wrong.
　　When dealing in commodities,
　　It's not your taste you seek to please.
　　I should not have to moralize;
　　Here profit is your only prize!

13/What's Your Style?

Style, as used in this chapter, means a characteristic manner of operation. There is a wide variety of styles used in trading commodity futures. In general, there's the style of the habitual plunger who is determined either to make his fortune or go broke in the attempt; then there's the commercial style of the trade which uses the futures markets to help solve inventory problems; and, in between, there's the speculative style of the trader whose profits enable the prosperity of futures markets.

Although successful traders enable the prosperity of futures markets, these markets do not exist for the purpose of furnishing traders with a livelihood. Futures markets exist for the *trade.* The trade consists of that broad range of business people who own Lumber mills, grow Wheat, raise Cattle, mine Silver, export Soybean Oil, import Platinum, convert Cotton, operate Pork Belly storage facilities, manufacture Brass products, make Chocolate bars, et cetera.

There is an unsubstantiated and probably fallacious belief that the trade uses the futures markets essentially for hedging purposes. In actuality, it would be inadvisable for the trade to use the futures markets essentially for hedging purposes. There are two types of hedges, buying hedges and selling hedges. A buying hedge is used when a product has been sold for future delivery but is not yet possessed. For instance, an exporter who sells SBO (Soybean Oil) to an overseas customer for delivery four months hence is vulnerable to a price rise unless he already owns or has commitments from suppliers for a corresponding amount. If vulnerable to a price rise, the exporter can purchase SBO futures contracts. In so doing, he virtually establishes the profitability of his overseas sale. A selling hedge, on the other hand, is used to protect unsold inventory from a price decline. For instance, a Platinum importer who receives a shipment may take months to sell all of it to his customers. During this interval, he can *in theory* be protected from a price decline by being short Platinum futures contracts. Buying hedges usually make sense in both theory and in practice. Selling hedges often do not work out in practice. In sharply advancing markets, those with abundant unhedged inventories are able to seriously bruise their less well-endowed competitors. A classic case is provided by General Foods.

General Foods makes many popular products. One of this company's most popular for several generations has been Maxwell House Coffee. During the early and middle 1930's, Coffee prices were so weak that the government of Brazil purchased and dumped into the Atlantic Ocean huge quantities in an attempt to shore up Brazil's sagging economy. At that time, General Foods was maintaining a six-month Coffee inventory for operational purposes. To protect itself against even lower Coffee prices, General Foods was frequently short Coffee futures contracts. However, as war clouds began to form in the latter 1930's, Coffee prices began to firm up. The management of General Foods was brilliantly alert to the situation.

First, management decided to terminate the hedging of its company's Coffee inventory. Next, management lengthened (increased) its company's inventory and kept on aggressively buying Coffee in the cash market throughout the war. Also, in supplementation of this aggressive purchasing policy, Coffee futures contracts were bought until trading in them was suspended in September 1941.

Needless to say, the General Foods management was operating in similar style with respect to its other products.

From 1939 till the suspension of trading in Coffee futures contracts, the price of Coffee rose from roughly 7¢ per pound to over 12¢ per pound. By the end of war in 1946, Coffee was selling for over 25¢ per pound. During this 7-year period of time, General Foods found itself in the happy position of being able to offer its own customers substantial concessions, price and otherwise; solicit the customers of its competitors with similar concessions; expand its promotional activities; and still realize handsome profits. Maxwell House owes its long reign as a housewife's favorite to the fine market judgment and splendid style of men whose names are now more forgotten than ever acclaimed.

How did General Foods' principal competitors fare? None had enjoyed the wisdom to enlarge inventories. As a consequence, while Coffee prices were rising, they were faced with the bleak alternatives either of raising prices faster than Maxwell House and losing customers to that brand, or of retaining competitive prices and sacrificing profits per units sold. One major Maxwell House competitor had been for years sponsoring the highly successful Edgar Bergen radio program. Tightening profit margins reputedly forced this competitor to abandon that lucrative advertising vehicle. Those who had hedged their inventories found themselves in even stickier straits.

A far more recent case was the Russian government's dramatic purchase of USA Wheat in 1972. Wheat growers who had sold their crops long before harvest and operators of grain elevators who had hedged their inventories were soon to rue their caution; and exporters who had sold Wheat without yet possessing it were soon to rue their lack of caution. Obviously, for the futures markets to serve as a profitable hedging tool, market judgment must be a concomitant of that tool; because hedging can never serve as a successful substitute for market judgment. In addition, with inflation now a way of life in America, selling hedges must be employed with greater circumspection than ever.

Of the many trading styles that compose CMA, the most conservative is considered the style of the trade. After all, the trade is using the futures markets for *really* legitimate business purposes whereas the speculator is merely seeking to make a buck from fluctuations.

Other than the fact that creating insurance policies is just as legitimate as employing such policies, it should now be apparent that the stakes being played for by the trade may be far more permanently consequential than the stakes being played for by the speculator.

Of the many trading styles used by speculators, *spreading* is considered the most conservative. Here, the speculator buys contracts of one month and sells an equal number of contracts of a different month in the same commodity. He is betting that the differential will either widen or narrow. Where the spread is put on in a non-crop-year commodity, or put on within the same crop year of a crop-year commodity, there is little prospect of substantial gain or loss. Where the spread is taken over two crop years, the gain and loss prospects become significantly greater.

Some spreaders enter the market for a different reason. A spreader may believe the market is on the threshold of enjoying a large move, but does not know which way. He thus enters the market on both sides. As the move gets under way, he expects to quickly cover the loss side of his spread and ride with the profit side. One may ask: "Why not wait for the move to begin and then simply get aboard in its direction?" The reasoning of the spreader is that his way compels him to follow the market more closely and thereby reduces the chance of his missing the boat.

There is still another style employed by spreaders. When a certain market is viewed as strictly a trading affair, it is entered with a spread. Then, as soon as the market moves a predetermined extent in one direction or the other, the profit side of that spread is covered. The expectation is that the market will shortly reverse itself and move sufficiently in the opposite direction to convert the spread's loss into a profit.

Spreads are entered into far more frequently by owners of seats on the various commodity futures exchanges than by nonmembers. The reason is that members pay no commissions and can thereby afford to trade for smaller profits. In addition, by virtue of being closest to the action, members are in a better position to capitalize on momentary distortions of price differentials between two or more contract months.

A final word about spreads. Some imaginative spreaders have from time to time profited from putting on spreads between two different commodities. For instance, a spreader may figure that bad weather in the grain belt will damage the Corn crop more than the Soybean crop, but that good weather will have an equal effect on the crops of both. Correspondingly, he buys Corn and sells Soybeans. Or, a spreader may figure that a building boom will stimulate Plywood prices more than Lumber prices, but that the absence of a building boom will have an equal effect on the prices of both. Correspondingly, he buys Plywood and sells Lumber. Or, a spreader may figure that another round of inflation will advance Silver prices more than Copper prices, but that deflation will equally affect the prices of both. Correspondingly, he buys Silver and sells Copper.

Because members of futures exchanges pay no commissions, they are prone to scalp more than nonmembers. However, some members have stated that they would be better off if they had to pay commissions. Their reason is that not having to pay commissions often induces them to *over-trade* and thus make ill-advised commitments their commission-paying peers would spurn. Scalping styles are considered relatively conservative for the reason that a scalper never intends to stay with a position long enough to face a sizable loss. Usually a scalper operates by quickly jumping on and off a trend. His objective is to take a piece out of its middle. There are scalpers, though, who operate to catch small turns in the market. The successful ones are invariably astute volume watchers.

Most trading styles are based on the search for minor, intermediate, and major trends. The successful trader is constantly probing for such trends. In the process, he will suffer numerous small losses, but will many times recoup these losses each time he is able to grab an important trend by the tail. Once aboard such a trend, each trader will operate in a somewhat different fashion. One may aggressively pyramid as the trend progresses. Another may pyramid conservatively. Still another may periodically liquidate part of his position in the hope he will be able to replace it with an even larger position at a more favorable price.

The one vital knowledge which every successful trader possesses is that, while probing the market in search of trends, he must keep his losses small. To do so, he will use either actual or mental stops.

The successful trader also realizes that he will occasionally be faked out of a market in which he had been right all the time. He also knows that it is not a serious error to be faked out of a market. The serious error is made by not getting back in when the market there-after proceeds to behave as he all along thought it would.

Many traders find it more lucrative, more to their psychological inclinations, and more exciting to play for trend reversals. This is known as trend-bucking as distinguished from trend-following. The trend-bucking game is considered a more dangerous and a more difficult one to play. It is only dangerous to the extent that a player gets stubborn and persists on retaining his position in the face of a trend that is destined to continue. Actually, trend-following is just as dangerous—to the extent that a player gets stubborn and persists on retaining his position in the face of a trend reversal. There is greater validity to the premise that trend-bucking is a more difficult game to play. The reason is: All things being equal, the odds favor a trend continuation over a trend reversal.

The trade, on balance, is invariably short futures. The speculator, on balance, must therefore be invariably long futures. This does not mean that the trade gets a bloody nose each time a market enjoys a material rise; for, during such a rise, the trade customarily buys heavily in the cash market and sells moderately in the futures market. It does mean, however, that the speculative fraternity loses more money on market declines than it makes on market rises. It also means that the speculator is psychologically far more equipped to be a bull than a bear. One understandable reason is that a price cannot go below zero on the downside, but that the sky is the limit on the upside. A less understandable reason is a carry-over from the stock exchanges, where the short-side has at times been stigmatized as unpatriotic. After all, is not going short common stocks tanta-mount to betting against American productivity?

Putting inflation aside, food prices are essentially dependent upon the productivity of one of industry's principal cornerstones—the American farmer. The greater his productivity, the lower his prices; and the lower his prices, the more comfortably we can all live. If it is unpatriotic to go short common stocks, which it is not, then is it not equally unpatriotic to go *long* futures? After all, is not going long futures tantamount to betting against the productivity of the American farmer? Not that one should go short futures just to be patriotic; but one should certainly not disdain the short side of futures just to avoid the unjustified stigma sometimes ascribed to common stock short-sellers. This illustration, of course, also applies to futures in non-farm products.

In the annals of trading, nothing could make more fascinating reading than the styles of successful plungers. Regrettably, the adverse tax consequences arising from the brief lives of futures contracts induce successful commodity plungers to go underground or overseas. Brazil used to attract American stock swindlers. The French Riviera now houses some successful commodity plungers and their families. The successful common stock (or convertible bond) plunger is treated generously by the tax code. So long as he holds onto his position, he doesn't even have to pay a long-term capital gains tax on his profit. The would-be commodity plunger, however, does enjoy one advantage over his common stock counterpart. Ordinarily, his killing can be made in a much shorter period of time.

Although lots of plungers ultimately go broke, plunging does not necessarily mean the extension of one's commitment to the point where insolvency is the only alternative to success. Plunging essentially means backing a play with the majority of one's chips. Philosophically, it constitutes a defiance of the adage about not putting all of one's eggs in one basket.

Habitual plungers invariably go broke. Astute plungers are those endowed with the perseverance and patience to wait for golden opportunities. An astute plunger who became legendary in his own time is Jack Dreyfus. He aggressively bought Polaroid common stock for his friends, for his clients, for his partners, for his mutual fund, and for himself when the stock represented little more than the unproved genius and vision of Edwin H. Land. And Mr. Dreyfus kept on aggressively buying Polaroid during those years that Mr. Land's genius and vision were being converted into concrete corporate brilliance. Many of the millions Jack Dreyfus made in Polaroid were later invested by him to advance medical science.

An ideal vehicle for the habitual plunger is the *put* or *call* option on futures, providing such is purchased from a reliable firm. A rapidly growing segment of the futures business is the offering of put and call options on Cocoa, Coffee, Copper, Platinum, Plywood, Silver, and Sugar. Also being offered are put and call *combinations*, or combination options. Combination options are also popularly referred to as *double* options. A combination option on a futures contract differs from a straddle on a common stock in that only one side of a combination option is exercisable. Options on the aforementioned seven commodity futures are being written for 30, 60, and 90 days with the put and call costs being equal. A principal benefit of such an option is that the trader's potential maximum loss is delineated at the outset of his involvement. Another benefit is that it enables the trader to enter a market less expensively than he could otherwise enter it. Recent scandals coupled with the high risk in writing options on commodity futures may well see this business soon outlawed in the United States. For the enterprising, however, it will continue to flourish in other parts of the world.

The most active CMA participants are members of the various futures exchanges. Rarely does a day go by when a member not on vacation fails to make a trade. Even those on vacation are usually in constant touch with the *floor*. The next most active CMA participants are nonmember professionals who devote most of their time to trading futures. Our friend Shorty Long would be typical of this category. There are thousands of such traders throughout the country. Most are unknown to each other. There are also those, retired from other pursuits, who have discovered futures trading to be a productive and fascinating outlet for their unspent energies.

There are countless active business and professional people who devote part of their time to trading futures. Engineers and lawyers dominate this group. Some frequent brokerage houses for an hour or two a day, or for a few minutes several times a day. Others operate exclusively on the telephone, letting their brokers act as their eyes. Many operate sporadically in the futures markets, but follow them faithfully in newspapers and on charts, simply seeking a few good plays a year. Partners and other registered representatives of New York Stock Exchange firms are becoming increasingly involved in CMA. So too are a multitude of disenchanted traders in listed securities, over-the-counter stocks, and new issues—disenchanted because the action there has been slowing down. Many women also trade futures—and successfully.

Most who trade futures have the capacity to develop winning styles. Many already have. The thing that defeats lots of traders is that they cannot resist deviating from styles that customarily win for them. To stick to a winning style requires patience and perseverance. Very few can trade every day and emerge winners. Almost anyone who has the fortitude to await those opportunities for which his style is tailor-made will succeed where his more astute but overactive peers will fail.

But even a winning style is no guarantee of trading success. One must also learn the proper management of his money. Most people find it difficult to sit on cash. Good money managers know how to sit on cash. There has never been a successful trader, no matter how magnificent his style, who was not a superb manager of his own money.

It matters much to men of pride
What they have done and tried to do.
It matters more how hard they've tried
To truly do their thing or two.

14/Fast Action Portrayed

Wars and inflation create economic turmoil which, in turn, tends to dampen speculative enthusiasm for common stocks. Labor demands for higher wages become more frequent and more aggressive. Government is encouraged to fiddle with price controls and price ceilings. Gray and black markets begin to appear. Corporate executives find it increasingly more difficult to plan for the future. And capital starts leaving the country. Such turmoil, however, enhances the action in commodity futures. If the past is to serve as a road map for the future, the *Fastest Game in Town* promises to become even faster.

Until the Russians came to town in the summer of 1972, Wheat had mostly been in a bear market since World War II. The year 1968 was typical. After a 3-day island reversal in March, Wheat went into a 6-month 45¢ tailspin.

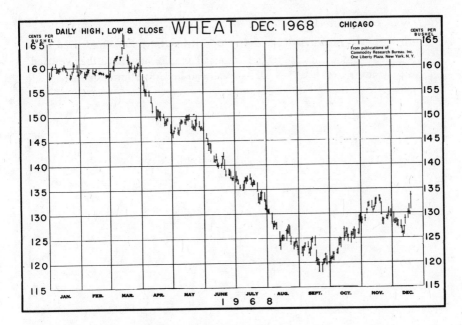

And then came the Russians!

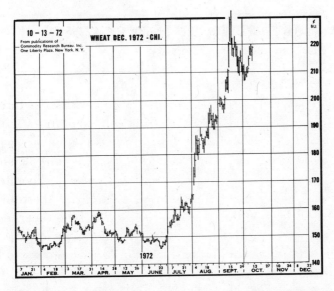

World War II sent Corn prices soaring to $2.60. Thanks to the expertise of the American farmer, even the blight over twenty years later did not send Corn higher than $1.60. As shown on page 164, the Korean War saw Corn rise as high as $1.95. The plunge in June of

1951 was occasioned by the nomination for President of General Eisenhower, who had promised to end the *police action*.

Although the Corn blight did not affect the Oat crop, it sure put life into this slow-moving commodity.

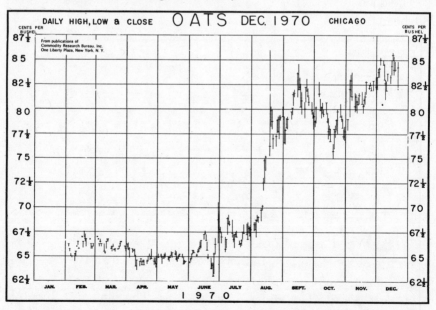

Whenever a bull move gets under way in Soybeans, everyone's

target becomes $4.00. Until 1972, the price of this grain had been there only once since 1954, and then just barely in 1966. Note the classic inverted V top.

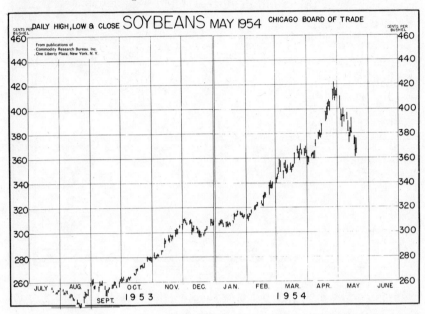

The 1966 Soybean Oil bull market was largely stimulated by the Soybean advance to $4.00. Unexpected bearish statistics issued

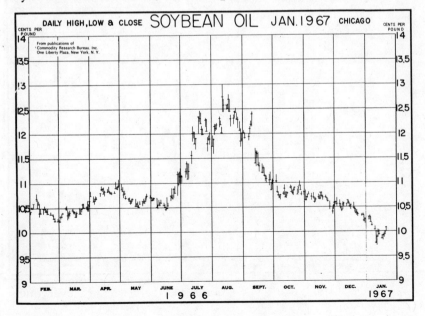

by the Agriculture Department in September 1966 caused a huge downside gap. Prices sank to 7¢ in 1968, but then recovered to 15¢ in 1971.

Soybean Meal prices hit an all-time high in 1972.

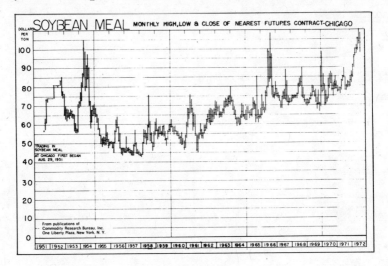

Rapeseed, which competes with Soybean Oil, is Canada's principal contribution to the futures markets.

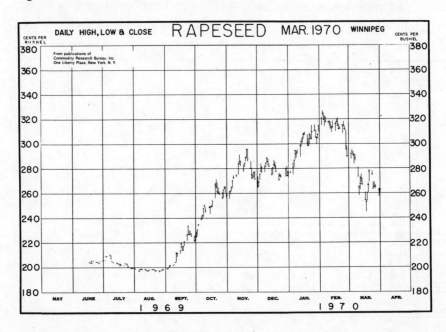

All-time high for Cocoa prices, in August of 1954, was promptly followed by a substantial decline.

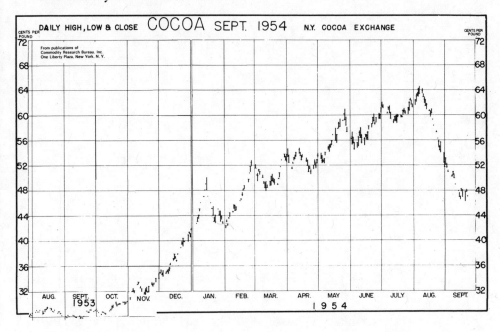

All-time low for Cocoa prices, in July of 1965, was promptly followed by a substantial recovery.

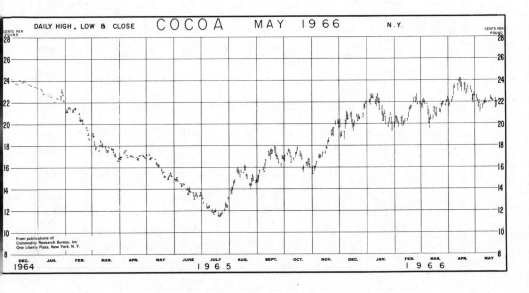

The Fidel Castro Sugar market of 1963 and 1964 was probably the most exciting of all time. Note the seven *down-the-limit* days in May and June of 1963.

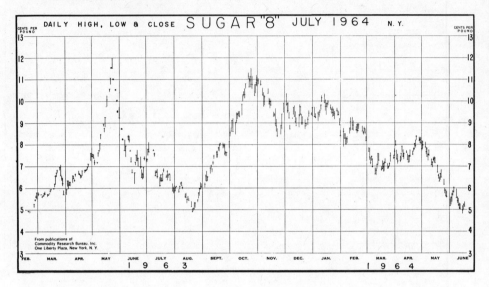

A 1968 December freeze in Florida sent Orange Juice *up-the-limit* seven days in a row.

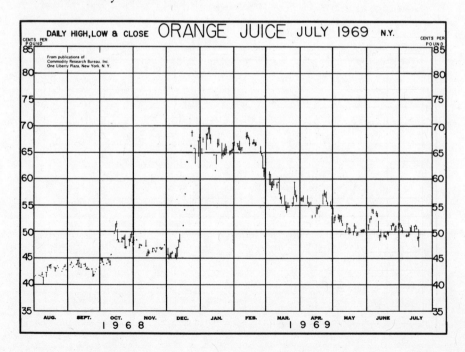

Notwithstanding an inauspicious beginning, May 1965 Potatoes soared to an all-time high price level.

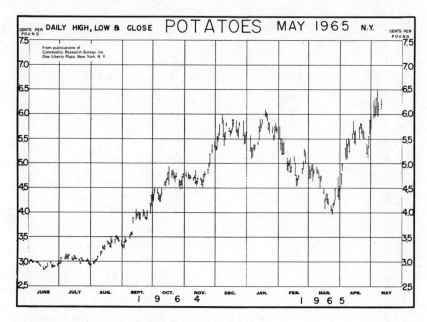

The Egg game never seems to slow down.

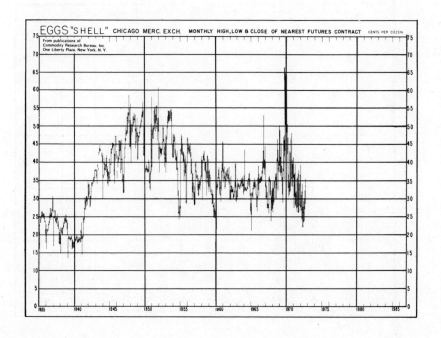

A two-month price-doubling move in Plywood.

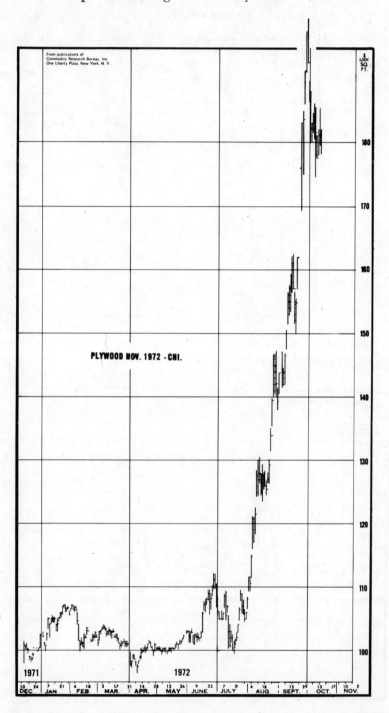

PLYWOOD NOV. 1972 - CHI.

Nor has Lumber been a sleeping dog.

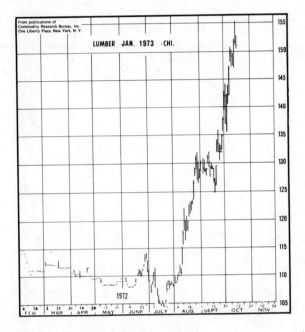

The action that catapulted Pork Bellies to number one on the commodity trader's hit parade.

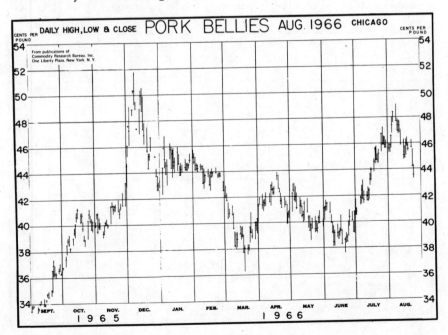

A seven-month bull market in Hogs—

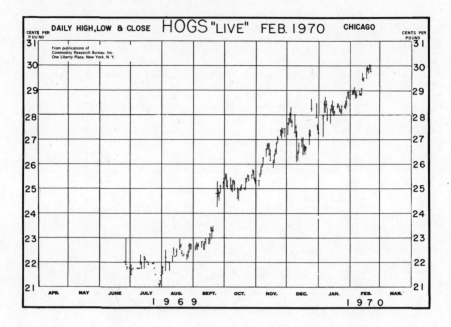

—immediately followed by a seven-month bear market in Hogs.

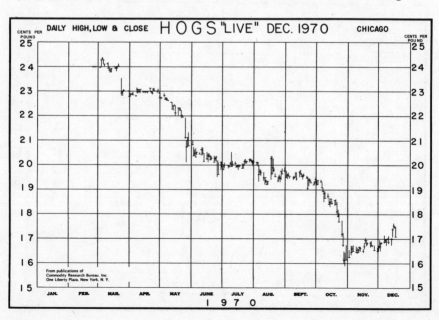

1972 saw Cattle prices nudge into all-time high ground.

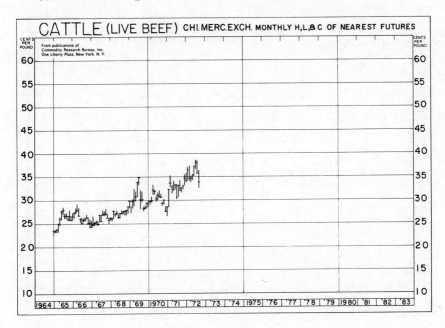

The resurgence of Cotton as a top trading vehicle.

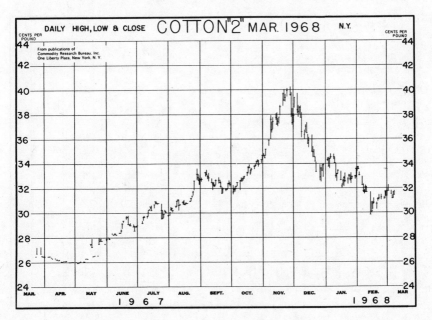

Of all the commodities, Copper is the most sensitive to the stock market and business conditions.

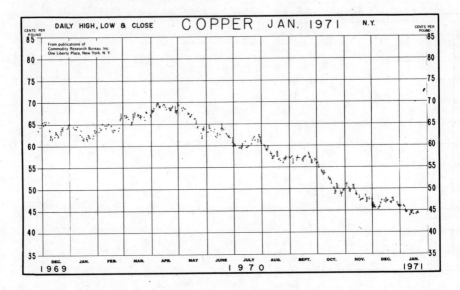

Silver took off with a vengeance in May of 1967—

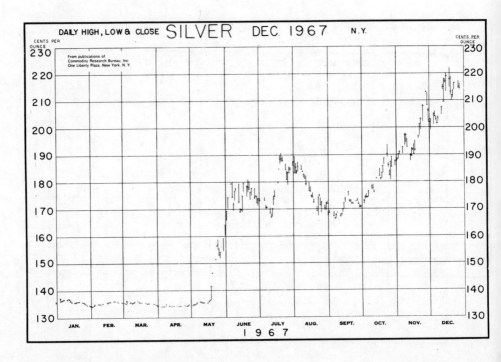

—and topped out in May of 1968.

But Platinum prices held up until April of 1969.

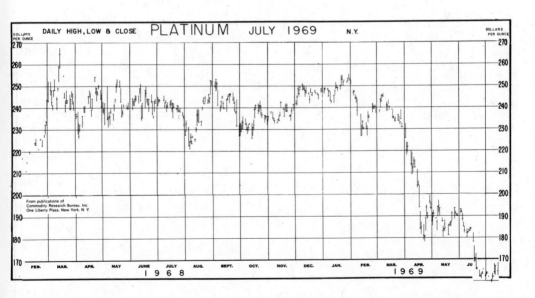

About the Author

A GENERAL PARTNER OF IRA HAUPT & COMPANY IN the early and mid-1950's, ANTHONY REINACH was responsible for that New York Stock Exchange firm's entry into the commodity commission business as a major factor. He, incidentally, made his first trade in 1948—long 25,000 bushels of wheat. His avocation has been writing, prose and verse, under his own name as well as ghostwriting for an unusual variety of people. He is the author of *The Nature of Puts and Calls*.